Christian Introspection

ROBERT J. WICKS

CHRISTIAN INTROSPECTION

Self-Ministry through Self-Understanding

CROSSROAD · NEW YORK

1983

The Crossroad Publishing Company
575 Lexington Avenue, New York, N.Y. 10022

Printed in the United States of America

Library of Congress Cataloging in Publication Data

Wicks, Robert J.
    Christian introspection.

    1. Introspection—Religious aspects—Christianity.
I. Title.
BV4509.5.W47   1983   248.4   83–1932
ISBN 0-8245-0583-2 (pbk.)

On July 15 and 22, 1981, in honor of the
125th anniversary of the founding of
the Sisters of St. Francis of Philadelphia,
I had the privilege of presenting two lectures
to these sisters at Neumann College (Aston, Pennsylvania).
This book is based on those lectures and it is to
this fine congregation that I dedicate this work.

Contents

1

On the Edge of Mystery

lmost everyone loves an adventure.

Yet fear and apparent lack of opportunity keep most of us from pursuing mysterious excitement. Generally we are passive; our pleasures come from vicarious involvement in the actual or fictitious journeys of others.

Moon shots are to be watched. Spy dramas are to be read. Pioneering trips into the interior of an archaeological dig are to be wistfully admired—from afar.

In a similar vein, the intrigue of mysterious religious power is especially popular today. We fill the theaters looking for visual "evidence" of the lost ark or the influence of the occult. Whether it turns out to be the hand of God or Satan's presence, the hope is that we will be given a glimpse of the unknown.

This particular fascination seems to stem from a belief that we cannot search for God ourselves. The feeling seems to express itself in such statements as:

> We don't have the right or the ability to search for God.
> The time has passed for such journeys; the Bible is history today.
> We are insignificant. Just as few of us will ever be spies or actively seek physical adventure, most of us are not among the "select" who can be involved in the *real* search for the mysteries and existence of God.

Unfortunately, this sad and erroneous attitude is all too prevalent. The fact is, we can and should look for God today, not only in the

Bible, other people, and the world at large, but also in the psychoreligious terrain within ourselves.

Whether we act or not, the reality is that each of us every day is on the edge of mystery. Each day we have the opportunity to look around within ourselves for the shadows of Christ. To avoid involvement in this search for the reflection of God in our talents and styles of dealing with the world would be a terrible waste. But pursuing a process of Christian Introspection can produce the real results that come to any adventurer who has the courage and stamina to step out onto unknown ground.

The following pages address a number of key questions which can help us determine whether or not to choose involvement in Christian Introspection. These guiding questions are:

> What is Christian Introspection?
> If the process is so beneficial, why do so many of us resist it?
> Isn't introspection too narcissistic and isn't it unnecessary for true Christians? Shouldn't we be ministering to others instead of indulging ourselves?
> How do we undertake the process and what can we expect from it?

As we address these issues, we must all arrive at our own final answer to the primary question:

> Should I venture into my own psychoreligious interior in search of the mysteries of God, or should I just accept the status quo?

Finding the answer to this simple question is more difficult than one might expect.

2

The Pastoral Care . . .
of Yourself

If we don't freely give of ourselves, we can't call ourselves "Christians." It's as simple as that.

Christ's words, as well as the comments of past prophets and current church leaders, direct us to be dramatically selfless. To paraphrase the late Fulton J. Sheen, we need to measure our generosity not by what we give, but by what we have left.

Naturally, this spirit of giving doesn't just refer to the sharing of material wealth. Reaching out and personally extending ourselves are actually forms of the ultimate act of charity. Shouldering the problems of others is at the heart of Christ's blueprint for living.

Yet in doing this, we are confronted by a very human problem:

> While we are extending our warmth to others, how do we prevent our *own* emotional flame from burning out in the process?

To answer this question, we can take a cue from Christ's style of self-ministry. He constantly took time to reflect on how the Father's presence was being made known to the world in him. For many of us, the excitement of the gospel stories consists in our being able to see this gradual unfolding of the Father in the Son. These stories can also provide the impetus to see Christ's presence in our own personalities.

Not to do so lays us open to real problems. If we don't make the effort to uncover the Word of God as it is reflected in our talents, we can't possibly nurture them. In turn, this lack of insight can lead us down an emotional dead-end street, resulting in either selfish narcissism or unnecessary martyrdom (what psychologists today call "burnout").

To prevent either of these unfortunate outcomes, we have to invest time in looking at ourselves and Christ's influence in our lives. One approach we can use is Christian Introspection.

Christian Introspection

Self-ministry through Christian Introspection is accomplished when we take the time to counsel ourselves pastorally. Therefore, to understand better what Christian Introspection is, we first have to appreciate the uniqueness of pastoral counseling, and distinguish it from both secular counseling and spiritual direction (see Figure 1).

Figure 1

type of process	helping focus	
	another person	self
secular counseling	person's relationship with him/herself and the world	self-analysis
spiritual direction	person's relationship with God	personal prayer
pastoral counseling	person's relationship with him/herself and others with an eye to the influence God has in his/her everyday life	Christian Introspection

Secular counseling focuses on a person's relationship with the self and the world, and attempts—through mutual understanding—to free that person from unnecessary psychological blocks. *Spiritual direction* is at the other end of the spectrum. In it we focus on a person's relationship with God. In the middle of these two processes is *pastoral counseling*. It's something that involves both religion and psychology.

With pastoral counseling, the late Daniel Day Williams of Union Theological Seminary said, "God becomes the third person in the relationship. Instead of being simply a dialogue, a trialogue comes into being."[1] So, in pastoral counseling, it's not the counselor and the counselee working alone. Rather, it is the counselor, the counselee, and God working as a team.

Wayne Oates, another seminal thinker in the field of practical theology, adds to this by noting that pastoral counseling is "sweaty participation with persons in their life and death struggle for moral integrity in relation to God."[2] He goes on to say that "the prophetic concern for doing justly, loving mercy, and walking humbly with God is the stance of being, an angle of vision, that makes counseling pastoral."[3]

Put simply then, pastoral counseling focuses on a person's relationship with the self and others with an eye to the influence God has in everyday life. And so when we turn the process of pastoral counseling around and become involved in Christian Introspection, we are then trying to discern the current status of our own psychoreligious terrain. We are doing more than mere self-analysis; we are viewing ourselves with an optical device in which Christ is the lens.

Christian Introspection is not merely discovering the positive and negative self. Instead, it is a prayerful process of discovery in which we search for the ways in which we have closed the doors to God's presence. The goal, then, is not self-worship but continual change in our self-definition, to bring it in line with an openness to Christ. It is this openness that is a response to Christ's claim on us. The "push" behind self-analysis is us; the push behind Christian Introspection is God. Consequently, rather than limiting our vision to the world at_ large, we are extending it through the involvement of the Eternal Influence in and on our lives.

Resistance to Christian Introspection

Generally, people are interested in themselves. Unless it is a sole preoccupation with self, this interest is natural and healthy. So the idea of looking at ourselves and Christ's presence in us would seem at least worthwhile, possibly exciting, and certainly somewhat intriguing.

Yet many of us often resist self-reflection. Though we may be aware of it, we often deny, suppress, repress, avoid, distort, and block out potentially valuable information. Such information might shed light on who we are and where we seem to be going in life; still, we avoid coming to terms with this material.

There are many reasons for this. One of them is that culturally, *self-examination* usually involves a good deal of *self-condemnation*. We learn in life that feedback from the environment can often be quite negative rather than balanced. Thus we wind up shunning "opportunities" for personal enlightenment at the hands of others.

A training program is probably one of the most obvious instances where this occurs. Those of us who have been in a preparatory program in nursing, theology, education, or business have no doubt experienced at regular intervals formal evaluations by our supervisors. In such cases, we were asked to sit down with the phrase, "Now, let's see what you have been doing." However, in at least some instances, by the end of the session we realized that the introductory statement really should have been, "Now, let's see what you've been doing *wrong!*"

Educators, directors, and supervisors who use this approach are often unaware of it. Rather, they themselves have been taught that psychological corrective surgery is necessary and that they should emphasize the extirpation of bad "psychological tissues" by focusing on a person's faults.

Such focusing on the negative and de-emphasis of the positive can become quite destructive. It makes us hypersensitive to the comments of others and even to our own thoughts. As a result, when people call on us to provide some "helpful" feedback, we often cringe and say to ourselves, "Oh, no, I'm going to be put through the wringer again!"

How many times has someone come up to us and said, "I'm only telling you this for your own good. You are a lovely person, *but* . . ."?

Even in psychology—the so-called "helpful science"—a person is often viewed in terms of a pathology or problem, instead of as a whole person with assets as well as liabilities. For example, someone will come in to see me and a colleague, upon seeing the person leave, will ask, "What's *wrong* with him?" instead of, "Tell me what that person is like."

Even physicians involved in holistic medicine frequently get caught up in seeing illness everywhere. As I entered his office for an annual physical, my doctor bore out this point. He greeted me by saying, "Hey, how are you doing?" Then he quickly added, "Oh, I guess that's a silly question; if you were doing all right you wouldn't be here to see me."

In religion, the same thing has occurred for years. Until about twenty years ago, the focus was on our sinful nature. It's changing, but a while back the whole effort was to get you to bring out what was bad while avoiding any mention of what was good. Can you imagine a Catholic going to confession back in the 1960s and saying to the old monsignor, "Bless me, Father, it's been a month since my last confession, and I want to tell you I'm really doing great!"

In most quarters this is changing. In fact, a case in point is Catholicism. Today, Catholic children are looking at penance in a different light. It is now called the sacrament of reconciliation. The emphasis is certainly different than it was in my younger days.

My daughter recently was preparing for the reception of this sacrament. She looked a bit down, and I thought as the knowledgeable parent and psychologist I would make an appropriate intervention. So I went up to her and said, "You seem a little sad. Is it about the whole business of going to church tomorrow and confessing your sins to the priest?"

She replied, "Yes. That's it."

I felt her apprehension (or I thought I did) and went on: "You don't have to be frightened of that fellow. What kind of terrible sins could you have committed?"

She looked at me in puzzlement and said, "What are you talking about?"

I said, "Well, aren't you frightened of the fact that he's going to yell at you if you tell him all of your sins?"

She said, "No. That's not it."

I asked, "Well, what is it then?"

She said, "I'm worried that I won't have enough bad stuff to tell him and that he will be disappointed!"

Times have certainly changed. The first time I went to confession I was filled with fear that I would get in trouble because I had done terrible things. Now my daughter feels bad because she can't make it worth the priest's while to sit there and listen to her.

Moreover, after most of the ceremony was over for her, I recognized even better the real difference between the vision I had of penance (i.e., self-examination = self-condemnation) and the way she viewed the sacrament of reconciliation (a chance for renewal).

When I was a young boy, after confession was over I think my whole group was—at best—relieved. In contrast, my daughter and her classmates left happy and inspired, and sang proudly, "Let This Little Light Shine." They all had candles and were happy to be together receiving a sacrament that meant they were close to Christ, that they were participating in something special.

Like our children, we adults today need to let our little light shine, but we're not sure how. We're lost. We have let the wax build up and fear pulling it away with a process such as Christian Introspection—it's as if we think the reflective process would be worse than the present darkness.

This is a crucial issue. If we don't take steps to abandon our old fears, find ourselves, and (in turn) find Christ, we are going to have problems. When we stop looking at ourselves and stop growing, losing our way is easy.

We are almost afraid of the childlike optimism that breaks through so naturally with the very young. But as Christ indicates, unless we become like little children . . . much, if not all, will be lost.

Once, a child was sitting at a table busily working with some crayons and his teacher said to him, "What are you drawing?" He said, "A picture of God the Father." The teacher said, "Why don't you draw a picture of Jesus?" He responded, "No, I want to do God the Father." The teacher went on, "Well you know, we actually don't know what God the Father looks like." Without blinking an eye the boy replied, "Well, when I finish this picture you will!" It's this sense of optimism that really comes through with children but not with most adults. And this is certainly sad.

In addition to equating self-understanding with self-condemnation, another reason we're fearful of embarking on a process of Christian Introspection is *shame.* We are filled with tentativeness; we worry about finding what is shameful in ourselves if we look too hard.

A lack of courage to face, accept, and move beyond our fears and resistances leaves us in the middle of a religious and psychological desert. Resurrection is not possible without Gethsemane. Awareness of how others are resisting fulfillment as Christians is not really possible unless we can appreciate how we are resisting as well. In essence, when we take full stock of our personalities, humble ourselves, see what is good and bad about ourselves, and accept a realistic personal view, we become free enough to minister to others. Certainly that is the Christian's mission.

In therapy I find that patients sometimes try to get me angry by focusing on what they perceive to be my weak points. This is not done out of malice, but is usually unconsciously displayed when they feel I'm getting too close to what they are sensitive about. If they can get me angry, then they have succeeded in diverting me from the issue at hand: their life and their problems in living it.

If I have not worked through my own conflicts enough to accept my weak points, then I will get angry in return; we will have a battle rather than a therapeutic session. Whereas if I have accepted my humanness, my pride, my receding hairline, my inflated ego as real factors which I must deal with every day, then they cannot divert me by pointing to them. Instead, I have the freedom to turn to the person trying to hurt me and say, "Your comment seems to indicate you're angry at me. Why is that?" Once again the point being made here is: Self-awareness and self-ministry must precede—and continue alongside—effective ministry to others.

Further resistance to Christian Introspection comes from an unexpected source. It's not the fear of discovering negative things about ourselves. It's not shame over what we've done, failed to do, or who we are. Rather, it is a *fear of responsibility.*

When I was ten years old I saw the movie *The Ten Commandments.* After the show there were about five of us sitting around talking about the great miracles, and we all took turns recalling them. The one which impressed us most of all was the parting of the Red Sea. The other four boys said how much they wanted to see a miracle. One of our group even said he would like to perform them. But all of this chatter, laughter, and banter came to a halt when I announced I never wanted to see a miracle. They practically fell over one another to ask me why. My answer was simple. I felt that if I were to see a miracle, God would expect more out of me. The same theme was presented in the movie *Oh God!* After George Burns, in the role of God, appeared to supermarket manager John Denver, the manager, instead of being overjoyed at the vision, lamented his fate. His feeling was, "Why me, Lord? I was happy just working in a supermarket. Now look at all I have to do because you have chosen to reveal yourself to me."

We've heard it before: "From those to whom much is given, much is expected." If we have the knowledge of Christ in us, we are expected to make fools of ourselves for Christ. We can no longer sit by as a spiritually infirm person, waiting for handouts.

This point is well made in the New Testament in a passage I couldn't understand for many years. There would be shabby, handicapped beggars looking to Christ for help and he would go up to them and ask the question, "Do you want to be made whole?"

Upon reading this passage, my reaction as a teenager used to be,

"What a silly question? Here we have these people with legs that don't work or who are blind, and he's asking them, 'Do you want to be made whole?'" The only answer I could come up with was that Christ had a sense of drama. I thought to myself, "He only has so many miracles to work while he's down here, so I guess he wants to savor the whole process."

As an adult and a psychologist, I can see Christ's appreciation of what in psychoanalytic terms we now refer to as the concept of "resistance." His question was a good one. Once the beggar is made whole, he can get excited, run down the street in ecstasy over his good fortune, but then he has to face a new issue in life: "What am I going to do for a living now? How am I going to contribute to life? I can't sit in front of the temple anymore. I must now take up my pallet and be more actively responsible for the direction of my life."

Today, a lot of people do not want to be made whole or free of their burdens, even though they seem to claim that personal power is the most important thing they could have. One person who came to me depressed seemed to resist any effort to become better. She always seemed like a silver lining looking for a cloud.

Finally one day I said, "Why are you holding on to this depression?" She looked at me. Her expression changed from initial puzzlement and anger to a sad resignation and she said, "Because I'm afraid of being happy. If I started to become happy, people would come up to me and say, 'See I told you, everything would be okay.' Then they would expect me to go out and really make something of myself and my life. I could no longer be dependent." There's truly a great resistance in all of us to come to grips with ourselves. If the locus of control is in us, then we are responsible for the use or abuse of our gifts and talents. While this gives us power, it also makes us more answerable for our successes and failures.

Three other intimately related sources of resistance to being involved in the process of Christian Introspection are *selfism, comfortable acculturation*, and a *clear recognition of our mortality*.

Without a desire to examine ourselves in the light of Christ, healthy self-interest and self-awareness can become self-worship. If cancer is the physical leprosy of today, then surely narcissism and unhealthy pre-occupation with self is today's psychological leprosy. Based on a distorted self-view, Christians can be led to a style of truncated individual "pietism" which could in turn breed a domestication of the cross and a noncommunal church structure.

This terrible trend is reflected in the appeal of popular psychology books.

> Self-help books are published in droves each year. It has grown into a multimillion dollar industry. Popular primers and aids for almost every aspect of our lives are available.
>
> One research study that examined the proliferation of parenting primers (K. Alison Clarke-Stewart, "Popular Primer for Parents," *American Psychologist*, April 1978) noted that almost all parents today read at least one book in the area, and that a significant portion read more than five. The report also indicated that the information presented in books is also available in articles of our popular magazines. The study went on to note:
>
>> No question is too trivial; no issue, too controversial. These experts advise mothers on the dangers presented to children by mistletoe and astroturf, baby bouncers and rectal thermometers, circumcision and Zen macrobiotics; they tell parents how to avoid raising a Patty Hearst and what to do if a boy likes pictures of nudes ("Don't worry as long as they're pictures of girls.").[4]

With such an inordinate interest in self, the fact that works are now coming out on the topic of narcissism is no wonder. Similarly, with respect to Christianity, it is not surprising that a book like Paul C. Vitz's *Psychology As Religion: The Cult of Self-Worship*[5] also has an audience today. Yet one wonders how much such critiques of selfism are read in comparison with their pop-psychology and utopian religious counterparts.

The danger for Christian groups is obvious. When people become absorbed in themselves, their groups fail to see their connection with the world community in light of the ministry of Jesus Christ. The result is that domestication of the cross and comfortable acculturation

are strong possibilities. The following sample of quotes from a statement by a study team working on the ministries of the Society of
Jesus in the United States point to this potential problem:

> Have we lost the conflictual aspects of faith and culture? In empha-
> sizing the grace of culture, in speaking its language, in winning its
> acceptance, have we become too acculturated? Is the "bottom line"
> of our lives no longer the imperative of faith, but the expectation of
> culture? . . .
>
> If we are honest, we must admit that much of the religion preached
> on the networks and in some schools and parishes is pious huckster-
> ism, an exploitation of religious yearnings in the name of grandiose
> financial achievements, feathered clerical and ministerial nests and the
> husbandry of power. The question we must face squarely is the do-
> mestication of our faith. In seeking the patronage of culture and its
> people of power, we must ask ourselves whether a terrible intimida-
> tion of belief has occurred. Has the faith been overcome?
>
> We must ask whether the Beatitudes have been relegated to a form
> of quaint pietism, whether Christ's vision of the Last Judgment has
> been ignored in a profound act of repression, whether even the suffer-
> ing servant Christ and his kingdom of love and justice have been
> made into mere metaphors. We must ask whether our inability to
> live the vows is somehow subtly related to our own cultural con-
> science formation.[6]

An ongoing self-analytic view with an eye to the message of Christ
can help prevent such tendencies from taking permanent hold. The
search for what God wants of us and who God wants us to be never
ends. In place of discern*ment* we need to be involved in a faithful discern*ing* process. Too often we mistake part of the message to us from
God as the whole message. We see it incorrectly as one that we can
embrace and be secure with forever. Yet these way stations in life's
voyage are not meant to be permanent retreats from the stresses of involvement. While we may gain a respite from the battle, the fight for
justice is not over.

There is an obvious difference between a sense of direction and a
belief that our wandering is over. The implication of this distinction
in terms of how we live our lives is clear.

In line with this, persons who really take the time out to counsel themselves pastorally have to face not only the hope of Christ that is tied to our faith in him, but a clear recognition of the pain of present living and our mortality. Paradoxically, as we begin to explore our almost infinite potential as people in love with Christ, we begin to see the finite crosses of our current existence. The denial crumbles and we are faced with raw reality. As we reach for the freedom of being one with Christ, we feel more keenly the chains of our existence and the "not yet" aspects of the coming of the Kingdom of God as reflected in society's injustices and our own inadequacies.

Even so-called religious and pious individuals may resist Christian Introspection so they won't have to deal with the conflicts that arise in becoming an aware Christian. As they tie their thoughts to the rapture of Christ's resurrection and his promise of salvation, they turn away from their own responsibilities in the world Christ has given us. In leaving things in God's hands, they forget their responsibility to use the hands God has given them. Having faith in God's ultimate intervention, while also acting in good faith as a committed Christian, is a true balancing act at times. Yet we must work to understand and follow Christ while maintaining faith in his ultimate intervention in the world.

One final block to our involvement in Christian Introspection is *lack of perseverance*. To illustrate this, I shall take literary license with the familiar parable of the sower in Matthew 13. I won't be looking at it as it was used by Christ, but as an ideal jumping-off point; this parable lends itself ideally to an illustration of how a lack of perseverance manifests itself.

In the parable, the seed which does not fall on good ground can be likened to the obstacles we have to fight in undertaking Christian Introspection. The seed falling amongst thorns reminds us of the times when our efforts to understand Christ's presence in us are met by self-doubt, personal fear, and a lack of courage to step forth and deal with some possibly unpleasant truths about ourselves.

When the seed lands on rocky ground, blooms briefly and dies, it reminds us of those times when we seem ready to understand and use knowledge about ourselves, but it doesn't work out that way. To put it another way, it is when we are faced again with problems or hurtful issues which we thought we had worked through, but which now hurt us anew. This can be discouraging, particularly when we feel we have reached a point where our personality has bloomed enough not to be bothered by certain issues, and we suddenly find ourselves tearful or angry when confronted by them again. In such an instance, we're upset not only by the fact that we are hurt, but also by the fact that we thought we had already worked them through. We find what we thought was baggage long ago left behind is suddenly loading us down again in the present. Such a revelation can be quite discouraging.

In the parable of the sower, there is also the seed eaten by the birds. In Christian Introspection this can be compared to the negative impact some people have on the fruits of our self-examination. On occasion, when we look at ourselves and produce some results, we allow outsiders to take this good outcome away from us. We get excited about something and want to share it. We go to a friend or family member; we feel good about our insight and resolution, and this person belittles or jests about what has filled us with joy. We quickly lose interest because that other person makes us wonder if our efforts were even worth it. In such cases, we have allowed our seed in early growth to be taken away from us before it has had the chance to come to full bloom.

Finally, there is the seed that falls on good earth and has the opportunity to root, grow, and bloom. In terms of Christian Introspection, we see our readiness to understand some of our own psychoreligious terrain. We then build on this initial understanding and gain a fuller grasp of how Christ is manifested in us, as well as how he is brought forth in our relationship to God and others. The positive results nurture us.

In Christian Introspection, as with the different fortunes of the seeds, each day we can encounter the thorns, bad ground, or hungry birds. All through our lives we must fight to develop our personalities. We never reach a point where every seed—every effort in Christian Introspection—will take root.

That's the problem. We constantly have to face our doubts, dry spells, and unsuccessful forays into ourselves. There will never be a perfect support group (a family, congregation, or group of friends) or perfect milieu for our growth. And many times we will have to return to old issues and sensitive memories (what I will refer to later as "healing areas") in our lives to work on them anew. This all can be quite deflating to us and our task of self-ministry.

On the other hand, if we despair and decide to pull back, a worse fate can befall us. For if we forego the pilgrim church and decide, psychologically and religiously, to set up a separate camp of our own, we will not only stop growing personally and religiously, we will atrophy.

No one ever has enough religious and psychological knowledge. There is no magical point where we have X amount of grace and self-knowledge on which we can rest for the remainder of our lives. I can see this in myself when I stop reading and searching professionally and personally. As soon as I do that, I start to burn out at the office. I think about going into another field. ("What do I need all of this pastoral counseling and therapy business for?") I want to give up.

The last time this started happening to me was several years ago, and I couldn't understand why I was feeling that way. Then something interesting happened as I researched and prepared a special lecture. While reading the necessary material, I started to feel refueled and better in general. The depressive shell which I felt was covering my hope and hemming me in broke open. I thought, "Gee, that was easy. What books was I reading? I'll just read them again and again." But, of course, it wasn't the *content* of the books. It was the *process of searching*. It was being involved anew in the professional excitement of my field and relating all of this information to me personally. I started reading and ministering to myself by asking questions like, "Who am I now? Why am I behaving the way I am in certain situations with certain people?" The excitement I knew as a young therapist interested in others and in self-awareness was alive again! Perseverance, self-reflection, and constant effort did pay off for me as a psychologist. The same can be said of any Christian involved in ministry to others.

Is Christian Introspection Really Worth All of the Effort?

Although we have noted some of the advantages of adhering to a systematic process of self-awareness, we need to address the issue still further. "Is Christian Introspection *really* worth all the effort and pain?"

M. Scott Peck, author of *The Road Less Traveled,* answers this question directly in an article in *Ministries* magazine when he says, "Any adult who wants to attain and maintain health must minister unto himself." He goes on to say: "As Jesus did in his ministry before he finally offered himself as the perfect sacrifice, the true Christian leader must travel a narrow winding and treacherous road between banality and crucifixion."[7] He clearly means that if you are going to be an involved Christian, you have no choice but to be involved in self-ministry and self-awareness. The alternative is disaster.

When we ignore the need for self-ministry, we can at the one extreme, run on and on with no self-reflection until we encounter burnout. We are then useless to all—including ourselves and the church. At the other extreme we can fall off the winding road of Christian involvement and find ourselves in the rut of stale faith. Either way results in the loss of our living faith and commitment to ministry.

If the talents we find within ourselves are to some extent the footprints of Christ then misuse or disuse of them are reflections of evil. The arguments in support of Christian Introspection rest firmly on this premise. We need to look at ourselves, with our talents and shortcomings, as part of our search for God. The Bible, the natural world, and our fellow human beings all harbor evidence of the Word to some extent. But unless we look into the mirrors of self-reflection to see what is religiously and psychologically there, we have missed a special source of God's reflection.

In *Basic Christian Ethics,* Paul Ramsey notes, "the first assertion Christian ethics makes about man in that he was created for personal existence within the image of God, and that Jesus Christ most perfectly reveals this image. The second assertion is that man is sinful. So fundamental is this doctrine in Christian thought that it cannot be overlooked."[8] When we do somehow manage to overlook it our personality can become exaggerated or atrophied and our uniqueness deformed.

Often our self-reflection does not delve deep enough to discern the difference between behavior that is prompted by the Lord and that which strictly serves our own needs. In other words, some of us become so enamored of ourselves that we fail to mature as people of God. There are times when the movement from representing Christ to representing ourselves is almost imperceptible. A typical example is the parish volunteer who spends almost every weeknight at various parish meetings away from his family. Is he really sacrificing for Christ or for the sake of his own position within the parish community?

Another example is the case of the young seminarian involved in the peace and social-justice movement. At the onset his motives and actions are fired by Christ and certainly his cause is just. Then slowly but surely he slips into the role of judge and jury as he speaks of love but with hateful condemnation in his voice. Basic charity and personal humility give way to irrational outbursts. Ultimately, he suffers, those around him suffer, and ironically his just cause suffers. In a sense he loses his way by trying to *be* the way.

Then there is the opposite extreme observed in those who seek personal revolution instead of personality evolution. Though they believe they are trying to change and improve themselves, in reality they are running from their talents as well as their faults. The baby is being thrown out with the bath water.

Ignoring one's own talents is psychologically wasteful. Religiously, it is a rebuff to God. To gain perspective, we need not turn our backs upon ourselves. If we are anxious about being hypersensitive, resorting to callousness is not the answer. Understanding when and how our sensitivity becomes distorted is. The well organized accountant who believes her orderliness is based on rigidity should not strive toward disorganization in order to cope with rigidity. Here, once again, the answer lies, not in elimination of the good trait (orderliness), but in trying to understand when concern with formalities, rules or minute details, causes her to miss the overall picture.

A final reason to be noted here in support of the worth of Christian Introspection is *knowledge*—not just any knowledge but the knowledge of our meaningful interpersonal surroundings. Charles Curran noted in his book *Psychological Dynamics in Religious Living* that the "genuineness that we communicate in relating to one another is based on the authenticity of the communication that one has with himself."[9] To know ourselves better is to know our families, congregation, local community of friends, society, and God better. To me that's fascinating.

In attempting to know ourselves better, we begin to see the cosmos in a clearer light, our defenses (denial, avoidance, rationalization, etc.) weaken and we see the world more perceptively. We appreciate others more and find that little things annoy us less. Quick categorization of people fades and we begin to see the special individual in each person.

The times when I feel real clarity about something are the times I feel closest to God. During those instances I don't dictate to him who he is; instead, I'm more open to his endless facets. No longer is my view of God immature and patently tied to his being the combination of a kindly old man with a neat son and a dove who turns into licks of fire.

Judas convinced himself that he "knew" Christ would never forgive him, and he hung himself clinging to this stubborn belief. On the other hand, Peter was open to more than the shame of his own failure. He was hopeful of the possibility that God was more forgiving than he could ever conceive. Such an openness led to further opportunities for good.

Many people may think that to look at oneself is very selfish. It's true that if the believing Christian does mere self-analysis it may be narcissistic and inadequate. Atheists can get away with it, but we as Christians can't. If we know God through Christ we can't just analyze ourselves—we must look at ourselves and leave the window open to an examination of God's influence in our lives. This may not always be easy. As Karl Rahner said in his small book *Encounters with*

Silence, "Why have you kindled in me the flame of faith, this dark light which lures us out of the bright security of our little huts into Your night?"[10] But now that we *know* Christ is the Messiah, we have no choice but to seek Christ in ourselves, as well as in our neighbors.

If we look only to ourselves, it is needless narcissism, and if we concentrate only on sensitivity to our neighbors we have lost our center—our focus of orientation. As Henri Nouwen aptly notes in his book *Reaching Out*, "It seems that the emphasis on interpersonal sensitivity has at times made us forget to develop the sensitivity that helps us to listen to our own inner voices."[11]

Not only is it really necessary to examine our lives carefully, not to is a slap in God's face. When we are interested in ourselves *in light of the gospel*, our human questions take on a higher form. As Hans Küng has indicated, "Encounter with God, wherever and however it takes place, is God's gift. Man's 'demonstration' of God's reality is always based on God's self-demonstration in reality for man."[12] To avoid looking for this demonstration of God in ourselves means failing to follow in the steps of Christ. Christ is the Word. Looking to Christ and looking at what gifts and talents we have to present to the world go hand in hand.

There was a bumper sticker I saw which said, "Christians aren't perfect . . . they're just forgiven." Knowing we are forgiven must give us the courage to take care of ourselves pastorally so we can then better minister to others in faith. Or, once again, in the words of M. Scott Peck:

> The love of self and the love of others are utterly reciprocal. We cannot teach knowledge we have not learned. He who desires to be a teacher must make himself his first pupil. We must nurture ourselves if we are to nurture others. *We must even stay alive for that purpose.*[13] [italics supplied]

Therefore, we take care of ourselves pastorally not merely to serve ourselves, but to be more freely responsive to the needs of others. We have a responsibility to nurture ourselves, to strengthen the community of God that longs for our spirit of service.

NOTES

1. Daniel Day Williams and Wayne Oates, *Pastoral Counseling* (Philadelphia: Westminster, 1974), p. 11.

2. Williams and Oates, p. 14.

3. Williams and Oates, p. 13.

4. Robert Wicks, *Helping Others* (New York: Gardner Press, 1982), p. 157.

5. Paul Vitz, *Psychology As Religion: The Cult of Self-Worship* (Grand Rapids, Michigan: Eerdmans, 1977).

6. Jesuit Conference, *The Context of Our Ministries: Working Papers* (Washington, D.C.: National Office, 1981), p. 23.

7. M. Scott Peck, "Self-Ministry," *Ministries* 1, no. 4 (1980), pp. 7, 8.

8. Paul Ramsey, *Basic Christian Ethics* (New York: Scribners, 1950), p. 284.

9. Charles Curran, *Psychological Dynamics in Religious Living* (New York: Herder and Herder, 1971).

10. Karl Rahner, *Encounters with Silence* (Westminster, Md.: Newman Press), p. 5.

11. Henri Nouwen, *Reaching Out* (New York: Doubleday, 1975), p. 26.

12. Hans Küng, *On Being a Christian* (New York: Doubleday, 1977), p. 85.

13. Peck, p. 8.

3

Healing Areas

Psychological difficulties are experienced by everyone. Each of us tries to cope with them in a specific manner. The way we do this is often shaped by our family and the groups to which we belong.

In this light, Christians can be expected to have problems similar to non-Christians. Yet certain difficulties seem to appear more frequently among Christians. These difficulties I shall refer to here as "healing areas." Though this list of them certainly will not be exhaustive, it should suggest the type of problems we as Christians often have to face. This material is also important because these areas are potential points of focus in the process of Christian Introspection. They will be discussed under three headings: imbalance, lack of clarity, and negative emotions.

Imbalance

Stress, guilt, depression, anxiety, and other negative emotional difficulties are often tied to a lack of balance in our lives. These imbalances can be viewed along a number of continua. The following are but a sampling of the more common points encountered in the literature on stress:

1. Self-interest and concern for others
2. Work and vacation time
3. Thought and action
4. Risk and security
5. Change and stability

6. Stimulation and lack of stimulation
7. Present concerns and unfinished business from the past

Self-interest and concern for others balance when we seek out opportunities to serve, but do not leave out the necessary elements of self-nourishment in the process. As we will see later in a chapter on "Burnout and Commitment," self-awareness and self-ministry don't have to mean selfishness. It is only when we put aside the needs of others to deal with unnecessary personal desires that a problem arises. Such an inordinate investment and concern with self is called "self-ism" or narcissism.

Work and vacation time are also meant to complement each other. For many people Friday night is only pleasurable because the week has been busy and productive. Work gives us the opportunity to exercise our minds and bodies. Some people are always faced with physical labor and experience little intellectual stimulation; others spend the whole day working with their minds and need a physical outlet for balance. The way each individual's life meshes together is unique. We all have to find our own balance based on personality and particular talents.

Those of us involved daily in a helping profession must be constantly alert—listening, analyzing, and then, often, still worrying whether we're intervening in the proper fashion. Even though we try to insulate ourselves we are always asking, "Am I making an impact in this instance, or should I try something else?" Consequently, I need to go out into the garden and plant without thinking about life's key problems. I must go out there and just *be*. Plants don't say anything to me, I don't ask anything of them. It's wonderful.

In terms of play, there's sometimes a feeling that enjoyment is to be left only to children, or to the irresponsible and narcissistic. Obviously, it's not. We all need "mini-vacations" during the day and holidays during the year if we are to allow our minds and bodies to breathe and find ease amidst the pressure of today's world.

The late Richard Cardinal Cushing reflected on this in his poem, "Vacation":

Break the tensions
of my nerves and muscles with the soothing
music
of the singing streams that live in my memory.
Help me to know the magical,
restoring power of sleep.
Teach me the art of taking minute vacations—
of slowing down to look at a flower,
to chat with a friend, to pat a dog,
to read a few lines from a good book.

Slow me down, Lord, and inspire me to send
my roots deep into the soil of life's enduring
values
that I may grow towards the stars
of my greater destiny.

To some of us the poem may seem "corny" or out of touch with the speed of modern life and the stresses of poverty. If this is how we feel, maybe we need to read the poem over and reflect on the possible poverty of spirit and motivation we are setting ourselves up for when we don't slow down and look at the beauty of each day. We don't have to fly off to an expensive vacation paradise to relax during the week. Instead, we can search our memory for happy times or we can walk over and have coffee with a friend. Relaxation is a gift of life that should be graciously enjoyed by all of us. Not being clear about this may cause us to stray off the path of Christian commitment onto a life's journey of Christian masochism.

Imbalances can also occur between the poles of *thought and action* and *risk and security*. Too much thought may lead to procrastination; whereas the action-oriented individual may become guilty of constant impulsiveness. With respect to risk and security, as Christians we should be able to risk more because as believers we should have within us a greater sense of safety. Even when doubts about our faith arise, we should still be more alive than a person without faith because we are grappling with such essential issues. The problem too often is that we see small r's (risks) as being the equivalent of big R's. This confusion leads us to withdraw. We try to hide within ourselves and our churches while people are suffering outside. This embrace of the status quo and rejection of the pilgrim church may seem attractive, but it's a false security. As Christians, as soon as we cease our quest for greater justice, truth, and love, our faith atrophies and our hope becomes an empty virtue.

If we are not careful, *change and stability* will mark another area which will be a source of undue stress in our lives. In psychology there is a rule of thumb: Avoid changing many things at once, but be open to great change over time. If we change too many things at once we can lose our sense of orientation in life. Change certainly can be good. Avoiding it at all cost, as some people do, can result in stagnation. Still, if we are forced to make many changes in our lives, we should try to hold on to certain familiar supports or undue stress can be expected.

Stimulation and lack of stimulation is another potential area of imbalance. If we are understimulated we become self-centered and fail to develop adequate coping mechanisms. Unless we interact with the problems and questions of life as they manifest themselves in the people we meet, we cannot continue to extend our horizon of hospitality to others who need our communal support. This can, in turn, lead to an increase in prejudice toward the differences of others. We may then confuse the concept of truth with a desire for conformity and "sameness"; if others are not identical with our group we will erroneously believe they are to be avoided, shunned, and feared.

Overload is the opposite of understimulation and this too is a natural danger. When we ask ourselves, "Are we involved enough?" we need to recognize the difference between quality and quantity. We need to have the courage to close our door to pray and think, just as we need to have the common sense to see that sometimes reaching a few people effectively is more meaningful than rushing around trying to be all things to everyone in a single day.

Present concerns and unfinished business from the past get confused in our lives every day. This is understandable. When we were young we developed a style of dealing with the important people in our lives (mother, father, peers, etc.). This style remains with us throughout our lives. However, we need to recognize the times we use this style with people now as if they were people from our childhood. Too often we see authority figures as our parents, and fail to see them for what they are and how they are behaving in the present. Also, because our parents and the significant people in our early lives were human, they made mistakes. They didn't give us enough love, or they smothered us with so much of it we couldn't breathe the air of independence when we were ready for it. They might have been too rigid, or perhaps they didn't provide us with enough limits. But whatever might have happened in childhood, we are left with some unfinished business in our personalities. We are left with stored-up feelings of anger, resentment, and sensitivity. As a result, sometimes we get tied up in the past and fail to see that we are putting pressure on others to take care of our unfinished business.

One student I had in class always seemed angry at me and her other male teachers. One day I asked her about it and she said it was because I joked in class and she felt I was being pedantic. As we talked about the situations she cited for support, we recognized that with one possible exception these instances were grossly misinterpreted. When we spoke about it further she noted that she was sensitive about males joking with her because she had three older brothers who used to tease her as a child and adolescent. Though she was accurate in her appraisal of their style of dealing with her, she was generally expecting it in other situations now and was acting accordingly. By understanding this, she was able to be more discriminating in how she interpreted current situations. In addition, she was able to see that some of her unfinished business was a desire to be respected and a wish to get revenge against those who teased her. She was also able to feel greater confidence in recognizing true chauvinistic behavior because she was able to view such interactions more clearly. In essence, she became more powerful.

There are numerous other poles and continua we can't cover here but which need to be faced and balanced in our lives as Christians. To uncover them on our own, we need to ask ourselves questions at those times when we feel pain so we can achieve a proper sense of psychological and spiritual equilibrium. Such questions might be along the following lines: "Am I too involved, or too detached?" "Am I too concerned about what I do instead of who I am, or do I hold back and not do enough?" "Do I aspire for such great things by my own hands that I fail to appreciate that it is only God who can accomplish all? Or, on the other hand, do I fail to try hard enough and hide my talents under a bushel?" These questions might be helpful in discovering the unique pattern of imbalances in our own life and subsequently allowing the unnecessary hurts in our lives to be healed. Self-understanding in the Christian motif can then lead to greater service to others, for in being freed from our unnecessary burdens, we will be better able to help others eliminate theirs.

Lack of Clarity

When I experience real clarity I feel really free. This is even the case when I see the complexities of an issue or stance which raises conflict for me. In our role definitions, for example, we have many inbred conflicts. When we are vague and have role confusion, we don't know how to act. Yet when we gain clarity about who we are and what our responsibilities are as priest, parent, helper, teacher, female religious, deacon, father, brother, or friend, we are left with an opportunity to set priorities and make decisions. No action or solution will be totally correct or satisfying, but if we have clarity when we decide, we will have a sense of confidence that will give us peace and strength when we need it.

To arrive at a clarity that is tied to Christian principles, rather than a delusion fired by our own needs and insecurities, we must prayerfully question ourselves. Below are several common areas we must come to terms with and some sample questions we can ask ourselves while praying for insight. These are offered as a possible approach when addressing points of confusion or vagueness in our lives.

> *Measuring personal effectiveness*
> What is success to me?
> Is it end results or the process that is
>   important?

Who is a good person with whom to discuss my
   performance?

Determining our support systems
Who is/are my family?
Who are my friends?
How well do I trust others and how trustworthy
   am I?
What are reasonable expectations for those I look
   to in my community or family for support?

Role definition
Who am I *now*?
Where am I confused regarding my role now in life?
What conflicts do I have, given my role in life?
How do I resolve them?
How do I picture myself now? (Am I still
   seeing myself now as I looked in my "psychological
   photo" ten years ago?)

Obtaining a clear picture of something is not easy. Sometimes we
shun clarity because we feel we must then correct what we see is
wrong. Still, seeking clarity seems to be a very worthwhile goal, for it
moves us away from the false beliefs we have about life as part of our
journey toward the truth and a more complete Christian commitment. No matter how hard the process, it's worth it. I must say that at
those moments when I experience real clarity I feel closest to God.

Negative Emotions

Three negative emotions almost everyone feels to some extent are
anxiety, depression, and anger. *Anxiety* occurs when we become fearful without due cause. The less clear we are about ourselves and our
duties, the more apt we are to feel anxiety. For instance, if we have
pangs of guilt because we are happy on a weekend vacation and think
we should be working all the time, anxiety occurs because we don't
believe we are acting according to how we *should* behave.

Much has been written on anxiety, especially in relation to understanding when our "shoulds" are tied to an unrealistic view of life based on a warped conscience (superego). As Christians we need to ask ourselves if our fears of not being good enough to others are tied to reality or a too strict view of what people should be and can do in life. Help on this is also available from spiritual directors, trusted colleagues, advisors, and peers. Finding the balance between being too scrupulous and not having enough concern about whether we are doing right can alleviate the toll that undue anxiety can take, as well as prevent us from insulating ourselves from involvement in those causes and stands which merit our attention even though they might result in necessary pain.

Books upon books have also been written about *depression*. For our part here, the interest we have is the relationship depression has with Christian goals. Quite frequently I have seen in the caring Christian confusion about the place of goals in our lives. Depression can be caused by numerous elements, but statistically in my clinical work I have noted that a common cause of depression specifically in Christians is that they let their goals threaten them rather than be a source of inspiration.

Too often, instead of saying, "I want to be like Christ and see his image as a light drawing me and helping me correct the mistakes I have made," a person says, "I must be more like Christ. I am not, so I am a failure as a Christian." A sense of despair results. They forgive others who try and miss the mark, but they can't forgive themselves.

Another cause of depression in Christians is a poor understanding of (to borrow the title of Rabbi Kushner's book) why bad things happen to good people. Many of us are so tied to a belief in an immediately rewarding God that we become upset when crisis or loss comes our way. When the crisis doesn't turn out the way we would like or the loss is permanent, we feel we (and sometimes God) have failed. The result: We become our own worst enemy and we compound the trouble with anger against self and God.

Learning how to turn the pain we experience as a part of living in a difficult world into an opportunity for growth can relieve depression. Yet this can only occur if we are willing to understand clearly that bad things sometimes unavoidably do happen to good people. Maybe we can't always prevent bad things, but we can grow from the pain they produce.

Probably the most widespread negative emotion for Christians, though, is unexpressed *anger*. When we recognize the terrible implications of this, it becomes an issue which we are urgently called to face. Robert Chernin Cantor in his book *And a Time to Live: Toward Emotional Well Being During the Crisis of Cancer* aptly points this out.

> Over a longer period of time, the internal consequences of unexpressed anger can be injurious, especially when disease is present. Diabetics find it much easier to maintain control of their disease by means of medication when they are able to express anger. Cancer patients who tend to be the most eager to please others, those who deny themselves a productive form of emotional expression, have been shown to suffer proportionately faster tumor growth.[1]

The awful impact submerged anger has on Christians is also worthy of note. The minister who swallows his anger under the false notion that Christian leaders never get angry is asking for psychosomatic problems or setting the stage for his anger to come out indirectly (passive-aggressive behavior). The Christian parent who has a good deal of submerged anger but is afraid to admit it may set such rigid guidelines for his family and others that he drives others away from religion rather than to Christ. The group of Christians who are so fearful of expressing any kind of anger that they fail to confront real issues and each other will suffer from what Augsberger in his book *Anger and Assertiveness in Pastoral Care*[2] calls "chronic niceness"—leading to a sweet, but quite emotionally dead congregation. The price we as Christians pay for unaccepted and unresolved anger is high.

Anger is part of life. Sometimes it's justified. Sometimes it is the result of someone focusing on our sensitive issues in life. We need to deal with anger as effectively as the other healing areas in our life if we are to strive to move the unnecessary blocks from our path to involved Christian living. Not accepting our anger can prevent us from being alive and spontaneous. Being sensitive to it can make us appreciate what fears and anxieties we have in dealing with others, and lead to increasing our opportunities to remove injustices without unnecessarily injuring the people responsible for them, or hurting ourselves in the process.

To accomplish this, proceeding through a number of steps may be helpful:

Recognition:
Be sensitive to when and with whom we are angry.

Acceptance:
Ask ourselves, why we are so angry? Saying we hate injustice or that the person who is the focus of our anger is a bad or mean person leads to little understanding about why we are so upset. When people ask me, "Well, wouldn't you be angry in this instance?" I say, "Maybe yes, maybe no, but different things make different people angry to varying degrees; the question is why did *you* become angry?" In other words, "Why did you give that person the power to make you so angry?" To paraphrase Augsburger, "Why did *you* make *yourself* angry at this other person, not why did *he* make you angry?"

Reflection:
By taking responsibility for our own anger and recognizing that those involved were not only guilty of a general injustice in our eyes but were also touching upon some unresolved issues that should be addressed (unfinished business), we can grow from the experience and dissipate some of the intensity before we try to resolve the problem with the people involved.

Action:
Once we are clear about the problem we can try to resolve it by discussing it with the individuals involved. Communication about the *situation* (and not how bad the person is, or the things done to us in the past) may open up a way to solving problems in the future. If it doesn't solve the problem, as is sometimes the case, we will know that we have at least tried. We'll have the basis for analyzing other similar situations that give rise to unnecessary anger in ourselves. The goal then is: Learn from anger and deal with it, don't deny or bury it.

Understanding the healing areas of sensitive psychological aspects of our lives is the first step in approaching actions which can be taken to deal with them. Merely saying "Oh, I guess I'm just too sensitive and I can't do anything about it," or "Well, I just feel too guilty to take time off so I guess I'll just have to grin and bear it" is foolish. Yet many of us do this. Part of the reason for this—as we have seen—is that we resist self-examination and change. This resistance and lack of motivation to look and act is really too costly. Moreover, it is not in line with the Christian message: Make the most of your lives so you can minister to others with all the talents you have been given and are being given. With this impetus, we now move to the process of Christian Introspection.

NOTES

1. Robert Chernin Cantor, *And a Time to Live: Toward Emotional Well Being During the Crisis of Cancer* (New York: Harper & Row, 1978), p. 48.
2. David W. Augsburger, *Anger and Assertiveness in Pastoral Care* (Philadelphia: Fortress, 1979), pp. 1–10.

4

Christian Introspection:
Interviewing Yourself

Openness is at the heart of the discerning Christian attitude. To know who we are, and who we are becoming, we must embrace the truth about our present living self. In doing this we throw open the door to the Holy Spirit with a continual act of honest self-examination, aimed at achieving a *total* existence that is truly Christian. We recognize further that the challenge to live fully in the Spirit will never be completely met.

Karl Rahner notes the following in his *Foundations of Christian Faith*:

> For a Christian, his Christian existence is ultimately the totality of his existence. This totality opens out into the dark abysses of the wilderness which we call God. When one undertakes something like this, he stands before the great thinkers, the saints, and finally Jesus Christ. The abyss of existence opens up in front of him. He knows that he has not thought enough, has not loved enough, and has not suffered enough.[1]

This "knowing" that we have not existed fully enough as Christians is not meant to be a source of debilitating *permanent* guilt. Nor is it meant to discourage us, for we can never blot out the grace God freely gives to us. Instead, this knowing is designed to be a source of motivated movement toward virtue and joyous union with God.

As John Catoir, the director of the Christophers, points out, "We were made for joy and there is in us a human faculty tuned to God's inner life of total joyfulness. It is called the soul."[2] By closing our eyes to ourselves, we move to shroud our souls from God's presence and the joyfulness he offers us. So in interviewing ourselves we begin the search for the freedom of honest self-understanding based on faith in Christ, and a hopeful commitment to his people here on earth.

Avoiding Self May Mean Avoiding Necessary Growth

Avoiding something does not make it go away. Removing something from our thoughts doesn't mean that it will go away in reality. It may not be in the front of our minds, but it is still tucked away somewhere as a worry. So, if at times we are not proud of our actions and so refuse to think about them, we will not magically eliminate this unwanted behavior.

The same thing can be said of personality style. If we don't evaluate both our effective and inappropriate styles of interacting, unnecessary difficulties in interpersonal relations might occur. Socrates said, "The unexamined life is not worth living." I would go on to say that living with someone who hasn't examined his or her life, may make life *feel* as if it's not worth living. (Those of us who have lived in community can attest to this.)

People who are not coming across appropriately are people who haven't examined the "whats" and "whys" of their feelings, thoughts, and behaviors. We fit into this group when we fail to listen to those words of God which are personally challenging and when we get tied up with the *unfinished business* of life, and don't even know it.

Unfinished Business

We have already discussed the notion of "unfinished business." We come back to it now because it is an active element in the development of personal problems and difficulties in communication. "Unfinished business" refers to those agendas we have with others from our past which can color not only the way we deal with them but also how we deal with those who remind us in some way of these original objects of our feelings and thoughts.

If we don't examine our lives, we may continue to misperceive the motives of others and confuse the messages we get from them with ones we received and gave long ago. This is not unusual. We must remember that the originally significant people in our lives set the tone for how we deal with authority, intimacy, dependence, and independence. Our early interactions gave us a blueprint for life.

By examining ourselves we can see if the blueprint still makes sense today. This is important especially because of the interfering role that the past can play. Christian Introspection and the attempt to review who we are now and what we have accomplished can help set things right.

Though being involved in a continual process of self-examination is not easy, it is necessary if we are to change the way we see and hear things with respect to ourselves. With understanding and disciplined self-questioning, we no longer have to hear praise as a whisper and criticism as thunder. We no longer have to gloss over the positive and gravitate toward and emphasize the negative as if it were more important. We can figure out who we are *now* and where we are going in the future. A very logical way to begin this is by looking at the concept of personality.

What Is Personality?

Personality makes a difference in people because this individual psychological structure does in fact make us different from one another. *Personality is the constant, unique way we view ourselves and the world.* No matter how well someone knows us, loves or hates us, this person can never view us as we view ourselves. Nor can this individual view the world quite as we do. He or she may come close, but never to the point of duplication.

The way we see or perceive the world rests on a number of factors. Heredity or genetic makeup, prenatal environment, birth injuries, and postnatal social factors are among the key elements which determine who we will be and how we will see things. Here we are interested in how people organize stimuli and how they assemble and interpret data.

Heredity is certainly a factor in personality. We are born with certain innate abilities and predispositions. People aren't created equal—no matter what the Constitution says. No one would deny that Wilt Chamberlain is better suited than Mickey Rooney to play basketball. Certainly we are aware that some children are born with a calmer disposition than others; this, in turn, has to have an impact—positive or negative—on their lives. Constitutional factors must play a role in the development of personality. The exact impact they have is a mystery.

Prenatal environment also plays a role. Naturally the role of prenatal environment is not so simple that if a mother listens to classical music during her pregnancy, her child will have like interests upon birth. However, we do realize more than ever the impact and changes possible during the prenatal period. For instance, we know that a female heroin addict may pass her addiction to her unborn child. We know that physical and psychological trauma for the mother may have some effect on the unborn child.

Birth injuries and postnatal environment also are obvious factors in personality development. After the child is born, what he or she encounters in life can turn the tide in a particular direction. We see how children affect and are affected by the significant persons in their environment. Parents, teachers, peers, siblings, relatives, older friends—the list of people who come and go through our lives but who manage to leave some sort of mark on us and our personalities, is endless.

Of course, there are only a few who impress us in a large way, but there are many who share in shaping our culture and environment, so that we develop interests, attitudes, and character traits that make up an exclusive constellation which helps determine our individuality.

When we examine ourselves, we need to interview our own personality in a way that allows us to determine its makeup and primary characteristics. In other words, we need to know how we codify, classify, sort, accept, reject, and assimilate information. Too often we assume that the way we view the world is "correct." I'm sure that most of us are basically in touch with reality and can differentiate between fantasy and reality. But because we are unique, we tend to select and emphasize certain aspects of what we see, hear, touch, and sense in general. This has to effect our perception, and in turn our overall understanding, of an event or situation.

A familiar game that illustrates how our perception can effect our understanding of something is to have several people watch a common occurrence on the street and describe it. The differences in the descriptions reflect various levels of observational abilities, and also point to the different things that spark people's interest.

Real-estate agents have known this for years. They will show two people a house and what those two people see will reflect their individual interests and needs. In both cases, the persons interested in buying the house will have different impressions of the property. They'll look for and see different things, or see same things in a different light. Their needs, wants, backgrounds, interests, all will come through; their personalities reflect differences. They will perceive it differently and emphasize different things in different ways. We do the same in the manner we view other people—and *ourselves*. Consequently, interviewing our own personalities and trying to determine who we are and how we view the world is essential if we are to have better control over our lives.

Going beyond Face Value

When you suggest that people reflect on their own uniqueness there is often a feeling that such a process is unnecessary: "After all, I know myself; I have been living with me for many, many years." While it is true that you do have a fine awareness of much of yourself, as time passes, many of our styles, feelings, attitudes, and interests become almost invisible to us.

When this happens, we may have an image of ourselves that is not really valid. We may feel like the same person, but we have changed. The funny feeling one gets when hearing an old tape or looking at a comparison of old photos and recent ones attests to the fact that we forget that we are changeable. Therefore, there is a danger in taking ourselves and who we are at face value. Yesterday's liberals may well be today's conservatives and not even know it. Many of the statements, opinions, and thoughts we express or have about ourselves are just not very accurate any more. Unless we examine them, we can be led astray. So the first step in becoming more personally aware is to take the time to examine our own self-evaluation.

Being our own devil's advocate is important if we are to uncover outmoded images of ourselves. When educating interviewers I tell them never to accept what a person says at face value. In the psychologist's jargon, that means not to believe the manifest content of a person's message. Instead, the advice is to probe deeper. In the same vein, we must not always believe the obvious about ourselves. Instead we must look deeper.

For instance, let's say that a man decides to send his son to a prestigious Christian school. His spouse asks him why, and he replies, "Because it would be a great experience for him." This may be so, and let's assume that it is. However, there may be other reasons as well. If he accepts his initial response at face value, then he will not learn anything further about himself.

In this case one other reason might be that he would like to share the responsibility of raising his son with someone else; in this case, the school. Also, the school may be his *alma mater* or a "name" prep school and it would give him pride to know that his son is a student there.

Such additional reasons don't taint the stated one, but they do tell us about the man's needs and thus shed further light on why he acts the way he does.

Questioning Ourselves

Asking ourselves questions about how we feel, the way we act, and why we don't do certain things can uncover motives and styles we will be surprised to see in ourselves. To accomplish this questioning we should be aware of some *basics in interviewing*. In order to simplify the process and make it more profitable we will look at the basics here and in the following chapter:

1. Different questioning styles
2. Taking a complete personal survey
3. Understanding the "advantage" of not changing
4. Jogging the memory
5. Problem-solving and interviewing
6. Checking out personality-style effectiveness

By reviewing the information contained under these headings we should be able to reach a point where we can learn enough about ourselves to become even more dynamic in our interactions with the world. Though the following introduction on interviewing concepts is not exhaustive by any means,[3] it should open up to us those areas in ourselves that are important if we are to deal with the Christian Introspection process.

Different Questioning Styles

How we question is just as important as what questions we ask. If we know how to question, we can uncover a lot more information than if we just haphazardly interrogate ourselves. We can see how this works on the many talk shows now on television. The regular host draws out the guests easily and deftly, while a stand-in host—even a fairly talented one—has greater difficulty eliciting information from his guests.

When we interview ourselves, we want to emulate the good talk-show emcees and develop the questioning in a logical and useful fashion. To accomplish this we need to know the differences between open questions and ones that zoom in on details and specifics.

Open questions are designed to do just what they purport to do: namely, open up a topic so we can view it in as unstructured a manner as possible. Consequently, open questions are general, unanswerable by a specific terse reply, and designed to elicit a plethora of varied material.

In terms of questioning ourselves to improve our level of self understanding, the following are types of open questions:

How do I feel about myself?

What are some of the traits I want in a spouse (fellow religious, colleague, spiritual director)?

How would I describe myself as a person (father or mother, priest, friend, female religious, worker)?

What do I mean when I say I feel that I didn't become what I wanted to in life?

I want to succeed in my vocation: What does success mean in this instance?

These open questions are designed to get us started, to help us begin thinking about ourselves and one major aspect of our life. This is important because if we begin with a question designed to home in on details or specifics, not enough information will be unearthed. To illustrate this, let's take the issue of "success" in one's career. First, we will look at a general open question and the hypothetical answer, and then a specific type query and the response. The person questioning herself is a senior editor in a publishing firm.

I am an editor at a good textbook house. What would have to happen in the next decade for me to consider myself a success?

Well, I guess I should start with the issue of what I mean by the word "success." I feel that success for me would be . . . well, that's hard to formulate. With the president of the company as a model of success and his position as my goal, I guess I would see success as being what he was at each step of the publishing ladder. Looking over his record I see a number of things which might help me formulate goals. It's true that he's a different person, with different talents and desires; I could never neglect my family totally as he seems to do, but I could benefit from what I see as good in his approach and performance.

He seems to be creative, well organized, and able to comprehend the nature of the tasks he assumes. (Good grief! He's bloody perfect!) For instance, when he was marketing director he jumped in with both feet and asked the questions that should have been asked (but weren't) by his predecessor. He seemed to ask himself: What new avenues can we utilize to spur sales? How do we reach existing markets better and cull out new audiences for our books? And are we utilizing our sales force and direct-mail efforts in a modern, efficient way?

But the president, in his career path, also had another trait which I picked up. Even though he was very involved and identified with his role, he always seemed to be aware of the parameters and possibilities of the next-higher position. I like that.

Now what does this have to do with me? Well, first of all, I think I have been so anxious about doing a good job as editor that I have not asked myself the most basic of questions: namely, what are the best traits an editor can have? Then once I figure that out, I need to look at what the next jump would be for me on the publishing ladder, so I can alert myself to the kinds of things I should know as someone starting out at that level—the philosophy and operations involved in being an editor-in-chief. Let's face it, my time may come and I may be felt out about the position by the publisher and if I haven't thought it through I will not appear *ready for promotion*. Ah, that wonderful phrase!

Now the above discussion flowed from the general way the editor posed the open question to herself. Suppose she had asked herself a more limited type of question, such as "What level do I want to be promoted to within ten years?" The answer would be specific: editor-in-chief, publisher, editorial director. Following such a realization, the self-questioning might continue with a general question: "What does it mean to be an editor-in-chief, or an editorial director?" In such an instance, the whole process of understanding one's goals in light of one's abilities may come to the fore. However, even in this case, the editor had to at some point turn to a general, open question to get to her feelings, thoughts, fears, and questions about her occupational future. Consequently, in questioning ourselves we must be aware of how we are asking ourselves to reflect. Otherwise, we may end up by grilling ourselves with a lot of specific questions which won't allow us to open up to ourselves, but instead will leave us with a whole list of short answers to specific questions and no pattern to follow. Confusion and avoidance will soon follow.

> Yes, I want to be promoted within ten years to publisher.
> Yes, I think I have the ability.
> No, I don't want to remain at the same level.
> Yes, I know it's going to be hard to get to be publisher.
> Yes, I do think it's possible.

> I'm getting anxious just thinking about it.
> I think I'll shelve the whole fantasy for now and just do my job.

In examining oneself, confusion is not only okay but also inevitable. However, when there is too much confusion and we begin to feel fragmented, there is a great temptation to just stop the whole search and put off thinking about it for a while. This is understandable. If it happens too often, though, the self-understanding process might never get off the ground.

To avoid this problem, we need to make the process as easy and productive as possible. One way is to question ourselves in a manner that will smoothly elicit the most information. When attempting this it helps to know that there are two basic types of questions: general open and specific limited. This knowledge can then be applied in our self-examination.

The process of self-examination is a difficult one. Yet if we do take the effort, we can begin to see how old modes of behavior and past interpersonal problems can interfere with current feelings about ourselves and our present interactions. Similarly, we can also appreciate the other forces involved in self-examination, such as motives, fears, conflicts, strengths, and attitudes. With this understood it is now possible to move further along in the process by making the effort to see *both* the positive and negative elements of our interactions.

Taking a Complete Personal Survey

A helpful point to remember when embarking on the road to self-understanding is always to take a *complete* personal survey rather than set up a forum to indict ourselves for isolated situations in our lives. Too often, when we try to understand our actions or some aspect of our personality, we are driven to self-indictment because our actions have caused us some pain or embarrassment. Now while the desire to overcome an unpleasant pattern of dealing with the world is natural, we should try not to get bogged down in just inflicting insults upon ourselves. This self-punishment won't bring us any closer to solving the mystery of our behavior. So in looking at an issue or problematic way of dealing with our environment, we must be willing to look at all of our motives, positive as well as negative; we must be willing to view our assets as well as our liabilities.

To illustrate how a person can start at a point of self-deprecation, but in the process of surveying the problem get in touch with personal talents as well as limitations, let's look at the case of a priest who felt that he talked too much at a social gathering.

Good grief. I really monopolized things last night. I feel like such a fool. I don't want to do that again. I'm sure many of the people thought I was a big mouth and a bore. I guess I just got carried away. Why did I ever gab so much? What's the matter with me? I'm really embarrassed.

Well, all right, I don't want to do that again, but what should I do? Keep my big mouth shut and listen to others? Forget it; it'll never work. I can't stand around with my mouth zipped and my finger in my ear. I need to chat. So that's out. Besides, I think people enjoy hearing me tell a story. I do have an ability to get things rolling. However, the problem is that once I get rolling, I turn into a steam roller.

I guess it's the old question of the happy medium. How can I enjoy myself, be entertaining, which I think I have the knack of doing, but not get carried away?

I think what got me going last night was I enjoyed being the center of attention. Also, one of the parishioners thought he should encourage me right along. It's hard to stop then, but if I could follow the old axiom and leave them when they're hungry for more, I'd fulfill my desire to be liked and be in the limelight, but wouldn't overdo it and feel guilty the next morning. Yet, saying I'm going to do it and actually pulling it off is something else. So, I guess I should look at some of the danger signs that indicate that I'm getting out of hand and overdoing it . . .

In the above case, the priest didn't just lament his performance the previous night. He didn't just beat himself over the head for being the fool. Instead, he tried to look at the whole picture. He tried to see things in balance and what part he played in the whole situation. In this way, he felt freer to examine the night. We often wince at ourselves and how we act. Following such a wince is a temptation to quickly forget an unpleasant situation rather than try to understand and learn from it.

If the priest had quickly swept the occurrence aside, there is no doubt that it would have recurred in the future. Even if he had made a vow to himself that it wouldn't, or promised that he would keep his mouth closed, it would recur. For one thing, he would not have thought the whole business out in detail, so he would not have had a plan of action that was based on a clear understanding of how and why he acts the way he does. In additon, he would feel so unnatural just being a wallflower that he would get tired of the pattern and go to the other extreme.

When trying to understand a personally problematic pattern one needs to look objectively at the situation. Also, let's face it, we are human; and erring, as we know, is a distinctly human trait. We have to be careful not to blow out of proportion silly or impulsive things we might have done in the past. All people err in certain ways. To try to diminish our own unconscious and obvious patterns of self-defeat, we must recognize the general foibles and inadequacies of the entire human race. Otherwise, we will not be supportive and forgiving enough of ourselves to feel the confidence to take stock of ourselves. Obviously no one wants to look within if it hurts too much and the only expected results are pain and defeat.

Understanding the "Advantage" of Not Changing

One of the questions we certainly have to ask ourselves when we go through the questioning process is, "What 'advantage' is there in doing things the way I do them? Or, why should I stay and act the same?"

Many of us claim we don't like some of our behavior patterns, but find them hard to conquer and control. We want to deal with them, but nothing works for any length of time. The list, which includes problems such as over-eating, lashing out verbally at others, and being late for work, is endless.

One of the most productive ways of facing this type of behavior and controlling it is to understand why it is so resistant to change. Or, to put it another way, what is the supposed benefit from acting this way? Even if the behavior seems maladaptive, it must have some type of apparent reward, or it would drop from our behavioral repetoire. For the purpose of illustration, let's look at the following interchange between a pastor and a parishioner he was counseling.

"I am so impulsive. I just have to stop being so childish. How do I stop?"

"I'm not clear about what has happened since I've seen you last week. Why don't you tell me about the impulsive thing you did?"

"Well, two days ago, I got a letter from Bill. He's the fellow I told you about who was supposed to get me a summer job in one of the resorts at Hilton Head. I've been waiting and waiting; he was supposed to be working on it. Then I get a letter telling me that it slipped his mind and that he was going to get right to it in the next week. The only reason he even bothered to write and tell me at all is that I wrote asking him to send me the details on the job he had lined up for me.

"Well, needless to say, when I got his letter I saw *red*. I was so angry I could have wrung his neck. Now, I know I should have let myself calm down, but I didn't. I just called him and blasted him over the phone."

"But, what bothers you about the way you handled it? You were pretty angry and you seemed to have good cause, didn't you?"

"Sure, I did. But, don't you see? I can't go around losing control of myself. I don't like it; it isn't adult. I *did* have a right to be angry. I know that. But I just don't like myself when I let my anger out in such a burst. You don't seem to understand. I lost control. I just pounced on that phone, called him and then cursed him royally. I should have waited a while, calmed down, and thought the whole business through. I think I could have told him I was upset in a more reasonable fashion. Now he's not going to bother to try to get me a position and I don't blame him; I wouldn't help someone who said the things I said to him."

"Well, we have seen this type of behavior pattern in you before. It still continues. You must be getting something out of it or you wouldn't keep acting this way."

"There is no advantage to it. I always wind up with the short end of the stick when I blow up."

"Well, be that as it may. There is some short-term gain or supposed benefit to what you're doing or you wouldn't continue behaving that way; it's as simple as that."

"I am being honest in telling you that I really don't see any benefit to losing control and lashing out. I got the letter and I just couldn't contain myself. And I should have. Would you have handled it the way I did?"

"The important thing is you handled it that way for a reason. Now, you said you couldn't contain yourself. I think the crux of the problem is that you—at some level—decided that you *wouldn't* contain yourself."

"You mean I could have held back?"

"Why not? But what would have happened if you did?"

"Nothing, really."

"Nothing really, but how were you feeling when you got the letter and thought about it.?"

"I was burning up inside. I could have smashed the crumb."

"Okay, that may be the clue we need. You were burning up inside and wanted to let off the steam. You didn't want to wait to calm down. You wanted immediate closure."

"But that's no good to me in the long run."

"True, but it does have a value. You don't have to keep all of the tension inside. I'm not saying that this is a behavior to be cherished. However, unless you can see how your impulsivity is being personally rewarding to you in some way, you will never get a grip on it. You can't have your cake and eat it. If you want to avoid looking like someone with a short fuse you'll have to learn to understand why things upset you as greatly as they do and live—at least for the time being—with the turmoil inside. If you're willing to try to do this; then you have a chance to change; it's up to you."

The above interaction can be duplicated by us in our conversations with ourselves. We need to see the reasons we behave the way we do. Just deciding that some behavior is "right" or "wrong" will lead no-where. We have to question ourselves as to what we are getting out of doing things in a certain way.

We may find out that the behavior is rewarding for us in some way now, or that it is a familiar pattern that we were taught to use in the past and we are continuing it without question. Challenging so-called ingrained patterns is not easy. We have to have a purpose and high motivation. Also, we need to substitute one reward for another, so we don't feel as if we are punishing ourselves.

In the above case of the pent-up anger, there are a number of things the parishioner could have done to help him deal with his anger as he wanted to do. By thinking about his patterns of behavior, understanding what bothered him about the way this person treated him, what made him feel good and bad about the way he handled it, and what the advantage would be to develop a new way of dealing with it, I'm sure he could put his emotions under better control.

Jogging the Memory

Sometimes, in an effort to view the situation in as many ways as possible, we find that we're stymied by a bad or foggy memory of what happened and what we did. This is natural because when emotions are high and our personality starts to sort material according to personl needs, history, and personal philosophy, we are left with a prepackaged version of what occurred.

This is unfortunate because the more that can be recalled, the better chance we have to take a new creative look at handling our lives and the way we deal with certain problematic situations in particular. One way to jog the memory is to see the panorama of events surrounding the event as a story.

In doing this we are able to defuse the negative impact of the situation and see it in perspective. If we just focus on the one point of a particular day in which we had a problem, it is natural that we would be foggy about what happened. After all, who wants to remember an unpleasant occurrence? However, if we see the part of the day when the problem occurred in context, then we have a chance to understand the whole situation a bit better.

Once again, let's look at a dialogue from a counseling situation and apply it to self-evaluation—let's supplant the two people with one person who is talking to herself regarding the problem in question.

"I don't know, I'm just a compulsive eater. I just eat and eat and eat, and I don't know why. For example, on Tuesday I ate like a bandit and I really don't know the reason. I've thought about it, but it's all vague."

"Well, why don't you put yourself in the situation again, but start at the beginning . . . when you woke up Tuesday morning. Just relate to me about what happened during the whole day. The time when you were eating was just part of the picture. Concentrating only on that won't give us an accurate picture of things."

"All right. Well, I got up in the morning and I ate according to the doctor's diet. There was no problem. The funny thing was that I even revelled a bit in the fact that I was sticking to the system so faithfully.

"Following that I went to work and put in a good day. Some people tried to upset me by piling on too much work, but I didn't let them get at me. I steamed a bit inside, but I ate my salad at lunch and was proud of myself.

"Then when I got home, it all hit the fan. I found out that the trip I had planned on with a friend was off. She couldn't go because her boyfriend was coming in from Connecticut, so she'd have to spend the time with him.

"Then, my mother called and started giving me all kinds of grief because I hadn't called my aunt over the holidays. I started getting upset and I really felt that my life was all screwed up and that I was never really going to enjoy myself. Never would I be able to count on my friends to keep promises. Never would I be able to meet guys. Never would my mother stay off my back so I could be a distinct person. It just annoys the heck out of me..."

Now it's pretty obvious that once a person got rolling and started talking about her day from a neutral point in the morning, the associations about the rest of the day poured in. While it's true this won't happen to us all of the time when we put ourselves in the situation and try to recall the whole day, there is a chance that we can remember more if we start out *before* the upsetting event. If the situation preceding the event doesn't give us a clue as to why things turned out the way they did, at least we will be given a push from a point where the story is not full of turmoil and emotion. Rather, we will be relating things from a starting point where things were quiet and nonthreatening.

This is important not only because it will help us jog our memory, but also because it is in line with our philosophy: namely, that self-understanding doesn't have to mean self-indictment. Just beating ourselves over the head for overeating or excusing ourselves for some reason won't be helpful. In the former case we are punishing ourselves, in the latter we are denying what we did. Instead, we should try to view the whole panorama and understand what happened. That's the answer, if we are to gain a good grasp on our life.

Problem Solving and Interviewing Ourselves

To understand ourselves better, we need to appreciate different styles of questioning, how to survey our personality's talents as well as its liabilities, see the "advantages" or secondary gain of some of the unpleasant things we do, and recognize how we can jog our memory when we are going over an event or situation we want to analyze. These kinds of actions will help us reach a point where we can brain-storm with ourselves, problem-solve and delve deeper into our personality and our environment.

Problem-solving in our own life involves the following steps:

> Summarizing the thoughts and feelings evoked by the way we have answered the open questions we have asked ourselves
> Seeing what points in the summary strike us and are worth following up with more thinking and reflection
> Looking for a pattern which may point to a trend in the way we deal with certain types of things or people

Let's go back to a hypothetical situation during one of our past summer jobs. Suppose, for instance, that you were a bit annoyed and upset about an interaction with one of the supervisors at the bank where you worked. You decided to reflect on this matter and after about twenty minutes you arrived at the point where you had a good deal of information and were ready to problem-solve.

You knew, for instance, your feelings about the issue and some of your thoughts about it and could take the first step—summarize the material. The summary might go something like this:

> On Tuesday I went out of my way to stop in and chat briefly with a supervisor whom I normally do not see and to whom I do *not* report. The unusual thing about the act is that I don't like this man; he is usually not supportive, does not appear to like me, and when I leave him I usually feel like I've said the wrong thing—no, I usually feel that for some reason I'll never be the right person in his eyes. So, why do I go in there to be beaten down?

With this summary before us we can then look at what is striking about it:

> Let's see. I went out of my way to get bopped on the head. What is it about this person and being unsupported that go hand in hand? If I don't say the right thing . . . maybe I hope I will at some time even though this seems remote. But even though it *is* remote, I guess I'm willing to take the chance. But that's silly.

Then the question comes up: How does this fit into the pattern of my life? Does it match anything else?

Well, it may seem silly if I take it at face value, but there must be some logic in it somewhere. Even though it's not productive, what is it about a rejecting sort such as this supervisor and my going in to see him that needs to be examined? Well, two things are evident. I am being punished for going in there, but somehow I keep hoping that he will say that I've finally said the right thing: that I am the right person, that he accepts me. Hmmm. A lot of people like me. Why isn't that enough?

Is this something familiar to me? Have I done this before with similar types of people who were in power and didn't seem to like me? Well, it doesn't ring a . . . wait a minute. Yes, he's in power and he doesn't like me. If I can win him over, then it means that everyone will like me; I will be *totally* likeable; I will have made it. But why do I feel that I need to be liked by everyone and win over especially those people who don't seem to like me? Why does that bother me so much and make me try to get close to people who aren't nice to me? It's starting to fit. I'll have to think about this again tomorrow.

Problem-solving is going through the three-step process again and again. It's a never-ending growth experience. In this case the summary, high points, and pattern led to further questions, but also started to help in the formulation of good leads as to why certain behavior that seems strange and self-defeating is undertaken. When things start to make sense, then there is hope. And it is hope that gives us the courage to risk further exploration and possible change.

Personality-Style Effectiveness

One outcome we should see from examining ourselves and the way we deal with the world should be the elucidation of the style we use to interpret and take in the world of people and events that surround us. Each of us tends to have a basic style, and the more we know about it the more we can control it and make it help us in the way we operate in and understand life.

Though our styles are peculiar to us, some of the elements of how we approach life are held in common with other persons. Because of this we can group people and say something about them. Two styles we will discuss as illustrations are the dramatic, inspirational style and one that is best described as organized and detail-oriented. At their extremes, the former would be referred to in the psychological literature as a hysterical personality, and the latter as an obsessive personality. But let's use the more descriptive, less pathologically oriented terms; in this way we don't have to think of persons who use certain styles as having emotional problems, but instead see basic personality forces used by a person as a means to deal with the world.

The dramatic, inspirational style we see most often in artistic persons, orators, and teachers who have a knack for motivating their students. These people have a flair for getting others involved, and impress others with their sensitivity. They describe things and also view them in an overall way; we can see them as "broad brush" persons who are able to view the big picture and affect others with their understanding. A drawback to this type is that they may not have their feet on the ground with respect to details. They know what to do, how to motivate people to join in with them, but they are not sure how they are going to accomplish their goals.

The person typified by organization and attention to details may not have the ability to inspire others and gain their confidence. He may lack the charisma to be a leader. He often doesn't have the ability to convey drama and emotion, nor to handle himself in situations where causes and sensitivity are more important than methods and techniques. Yet this type of individual may be a meticulous organizer, a doer, and a detailed planner.

In politics, some people have compared the two styles in terms of Ted Kennedy and Jimmy Carter. Kennedy has a dramatic style able to capture the attention of many talented and dedicated people—but try to tie him down, and he hesitates. Carter, on the other hand, is someone who failed to sweep people and Congress off their feet, but who could provide details of how things should be approached and what factors are involved.

Each style has its drawbacks and advantages; in some instances, one style may be more appropriate than the other. Naturally, in politics we would hope to have someone who could both motivate and be aware of the specific approaches. However, in getting our tax returns filled out, we would probably do better with an organized, detail-oriented person who is only somewhat creative than with a hysterical individual who doesn't pay enough attention to specifics and leads us to tax court with little or no defense.

Another important point about our styles is that they are designed to help us interpret the world. We use them as means to an end. When they become an end in themselves, then we have to do something to correct the situation.

In terms of the two personality styles we have been discussing—those who make sense out of the world by paying attention to detail and organization, and those who are interested in feelings, impressions, and the drama of life—if the styles become ends in themselves and become exaggerated, then they will defeat their user.

Suppose it is a nice spring day and two such individuals look out the window. If the person interested in specifics becomes too detail-oriented and begins counting the leaves on each tree, he will not be able to appreciate the whole scene. Instead, he will be bogged down forever in details.

On the other hand, if the other person is so enraptured with the color and texture of the trees and grass that he loses touch with reality, he also will be deprived of the true picture.

Although we have probably not experienced an exaggeration of our style to the extent of the hypothetical situation above, there are times when the *way* we do things actually gets out of hand. We get anxious and become so concerned about style that we lose perspective. Rather than our style facilitating our interaction with the world, it gets in our way and we stumble over it. Through reflection and efforts at self-understanding we can reduce the impact of such instances. We'll see patterns that determine when and why we get carried away. Knowing this can help, especially if we don't jump to the conclusion that we have to change the way we deal with everything.

Our styles are probably good ones in most instances. They are helpful and make sense in terms of who we are as persons and what we do occupationally and socially. Yet if we can understand when our style helps and when it hinders, we have the jump on making the best use of our personality. The talents given us by God won't become distorted, but will provide us with a route to help those in need.

NOTES

1. Karl Rahner, *Foundations of Christian Faith* (New York: Crossroad, 1978), p. 2.
2. John Catoir, *Enjoy the Lord* (New York: The Christophers, 1978), p. ix.
3. For those persons interested in a further guide to interviewing, the author has written *Helping Others: Ways of Listening, Sharing and Counseling* (New York: Gardner Press, 1982).

5

Christian Introspection:
Structured Self-Evaluation

Systematic, continual self-evaluation, with an eye to the influence of God in our lives, is at the basis of Christian Introspection. In addition to knowing how to interview our own personalities, having a *structured* approach to self-examination may also be helpful. When we interview ourselves in an effort to uncover cognitive and affectual styles, the chances are we may miss or (unconsciously) avoid some area. Therefore, to aid in the discerning process of finding out who we are and who we are becoming, a sentence-completion form has been developed and provided here for our use.

Christian Introspection Sentence Completion Form

A sentence-completion form is a type of psychological-evaluation procedure. This approach presents vague stimuli to a person, who then responds in accordance with his or her own perception of the stimuli. There are no right or wrong answers. Rather, the way a person makes sense out of the stimuli tells us something about how that person feels and thinks. If the individual takes the opportunity to be as open and honest as possible, the sentence-completion form can provide a springboard to real understanding and insight into aspects of that person's personality. On the other hand, those individuals who are defensive and try to coach their answers or be vague will end up with little helpful information other than the conclusion that they are defensive.

This has been developed by the author for use by persons who want to try to understand themselves in light of God's *continuing* call for them. Consequently, the form is designed to cover many areas, including those elements which touch upon the person's relationship with God and the church. In this light, its use in conjunction with personal Christian self-analysis is logical, as is its use as a catalyst to self-understanding by leaders in religious formation, retreat masters, spiritual directors, discernment guides, and pastoral counselors.

Another value in its use is that it provides a record of our thoughts and feelings so we can go back to them again and again. Once we have our original impressions down on paper, our censoring mind cannot change what we have written and our memory cannot distort them as easily. Also, re-examining ourselves is of value when we have an original copy of some previous responses. This value is not so much in assessing the "progress" we have made, as in discovering what additional thoughts we have about certain issues.

Let us now proceed to the *Christian Introspection Sentence Completion Form* and fill it out.

Christian Introspection
Sentence Completion Form*

Instructions: Find a quiet, comfortable, and private place, and following a brief prayer for inspiration from the Holy Spirit, finish the form according to the directions provided.

Below are 75 partly completed sentences. Read each phrase and complete it by writing the first thing that comes to your mind. Once you complete a page, do not turn back to it or refer to it when working on other pages. Work as quickly as you can.

1. I look forward to

2. If only the church

3. My family

4. When the odds are against me

5. The way to build community

6. My mother seldom

7. Friends don't

8. A superior

9. My most important goal

10. I wish I could forget

11. I would do anything to

12. I wish I could change

13. The most important option I'm considering in my life

14. When I was younger

15. I see God as

16. I read the Bible

17. I am embarrassed to say I'm afraid of

18. As my epitaph I would want it said of me that

19. My father rarely

20. People think I won't, but actually I really can't

21. God has been working in me by

22. If I were in charge

23. I actually am able to

24. An ideal woman

25. Nothing would bother me if

26. I have responded to God today

27. My feelings

28. A perfect man

29. God tells me

30. I am really stubborn about

31. When I am 75 years old

32. The Holy Spirit

33. I really feel guilty when

34. My special talent

35. I believe God is telling me to

36. Sex

37. What I like least about myself

38. The spiritual gift God recently gave me

39. Anger is

40. No one knows that I want to

41. It's embarrassing for me

42. My father and I

43. God seems to be leading me

44. Families like mine

45. I'm very sensitive about

46. I feel fully alive when

47. Sometimes I wonder if

48. I believe my attitude is enlightened by God when

49. My mother

50. I should never have

51. My expectations about Christian community

52. My conscience

53. I really need to

54. I seek to evangelize myself by

55. I'm out of place

56. I'm full of joy when

57. A full Christian apostolate for me would include

58. I know it doesn't make sense, but I feel hurt when

59. I feel closest to God when I

60. Subtle sinfulness

61. The last time I felt depressed

62. When I give orders to others

63. Christ is alive in me

64. In my work I get along very well with

65. I think people like me

66. I really miss

67. What I'm now struggling with most

68. I wish I could laugh at myself when

69. Sometimes I feel compelled to

70. The person who aggravates me most

71. My faith is different now

72. I am not willing to

73. I drink alcoholic beverages

74. The scripture passage I like most

75. A person in my life who really made a difference was

PLEASE DO NOT READ THE NEXT SECTION UNTIL AFTER
YOU HAVE FINISHED THE CHRISTIAN INTROSPECTION
SENTENCE COMPLETION FORM.

REVIEWING OUR RESPONSES

Self-understanding, not self-indictment, is at the basis of the interpretation of the sentence-completion form. So, in looking at the answers on your own form (or in those instances where you are helping others examine theirs), great caution should be taken in attempting interpretations. Even the most experienced psychologist can make an incorrect interpretation of an answer on a projective device such as a sentence-completion form. Therefore, if we are using the form for our own purposes or to help others, the answers provided are only meant to be employed as a springboard for further discussion as to what the answer might mean, what can be associated with each listed response, and what some possible implications of the answer are in light of Christian living.

To assist in this process, there is a listing in this chapter of *some* of the factors which each sentence completion may tap, as well as the purpose for its inclusion in the form.

The steps to reviewing the form include the following:

1. Reflect on the following theme for a few moments: "The psychoreligious terrain within me contains talents that are joyful gifts from God and sinful tendencies that come from my exaggerating or avoiding nurturance of them. In knowing myself more clearly I hope to become more open to the nearness of God and my attachment to the community of people with whom I interact each day. This knowledge is not meant to be a source of *permanent* guilt or narcissism. Rather by embracing my personal shortcomings, I am opening the door to appreciate what is beautiful about me. This is done so that any temporary guilt may lead to action, and any healthy self-appreciation may lead to my better extending myself to others in the spirit of love."

2. Read each answer and think about the meaning of what you have written. (A narrative of our associations may be written for each answer as a record to look back on later.) The pace of this process will depend upon each individual; sometimes we may spend a good deal of time on a particular response that touches a personal chord in our lives at this time.

3. Read the Individual Question Review Guide that follows for a list of key elements that the sentence might tap and any comments written about its purpose and the method of evaluating it. (This list is provided later in this chapter; do not read the author's comments until you have first completed steps 1 and 2.)

4. Reflect again on what you have written in light of the author's comments.

5. (Optional) Review your sentence-completion form or thoughts about it with someone (preferably a mentor who is familiar with the form) so that you can get further—possibly more objective—input.

6. Look for any patterns in your answers.

7. Formulate a plan of action as to how to deal with the information so that it can be implemented in the service of personal (psychological and religious) growth, based on what God seems to be calling you to do in your daily life.

8. Use the Individual Question Review Guide and the success/failures experienced in responding to the plan as a means of further self-understanding. (A word of caution: At this step there is a natural tendency to indict oneself because of perceived failures; such guilt is fruitless. Instead, a productive response is to try to understand our obstacles to dealing with life more fully, so we can continue our efforts to remove them.)

Individual Question Review Guide

1. This future-oriented sentence taps our level of hope or despair, as well as the reasons underlying it. Another point to note is whether the answer is very vague or open-ended on the one hand, or very concrete and specific on the other. The topic of this sentence is a good one for personal reflection and discussion with others. (Is hope founded on Christ? Do we feel abandoned? Are our hopes mature ones? Are they selfish? Have we lost our sense of direction? Are we so busy hoping for the future that we have lost a sense of interest in and responsibility for our current situation?

2. Disappointment with the organized community of Christians and possibly the religious hierarchy are dealt with here. The needs we have that we feel can be helped by the church may also be uncovered, as well as the resentment and limits we feel that organized religion puts on us. The level of realism of the hope and the subject matter ("If only the church would *be more concerned with stopping the nuclear arms race*") should be looked at as well.

3. This very open-ended phrase deals with the family. It can be used as an entree to thoughts and feelings about how our family treats and has treated us. Since self-esteem and self-confidence are tied to the way our genetic family treated us, this sentence is an important one to think about and associate with. For those of us who are married, this sentence may be completed with respect to how we feel about our family through marriage. Also, if our family or origin was not a very secure and happy one, then our expectations of and need for community life now and in the future might surface.

4. Styles of defense are usually uncovered in this sentence. (Do we withdraw or fight on? Do we become depressed or angry?) Also, some feelings about how effectively one deals with adversity can come up by reflecting on our style of completing this sentence.

5. Our thoughts about community, our community needs and the way we would provide leadership are several of the themes to look for here. (This question and no. 3 are important questions for those entering a religious community.)

6. Thoughts about mother as well as possible early problems in nurturance frequently come up here ("My mother seldom *showed affection.*") In addition, we may see our mother as a role model ("My mother seldom *thought of herself; she always put the children and my father first.*")

7. Expectations of friends and the points which we are sensitive about in maintaining friendship may be noted. Our feelings about friendship, as well as how maturely we view interpersonal relations, can come out of reflection on this answer and a discussion of our thoughts with a trusted colleague or mentor (see step 5 above).

8. Feelings and thoughts about authority figures and early parental images come through in this sentence completion. What a superior should and should *not* be are worth exploring in our minds.

9. This general partial sentence opens the door to our looking at what we really want from ourselves and the world at this point in life. Noting the level of specificity or generality of the answer is important. If the answer is too specific, have we closed the door to greater issues? If it is too general, are we avoiding coming to grasp with the formulation of specific plans of reaching it, or do we merely need to articulate our "sub-goals" and methods more clearly at this point?

10. Guilt and feelings of inadequacy and embarrassment about past thoughts, feelings, or actions on our part or the part of others are noted here. This opens up those areas of sadness, anger, or self-deprecation that still need healing.

11. This open-ended sentence can tap an array of things. It frequently points to something we consider very important or pressing in our lives.

12. In looking at what we want to change, the locus of the change is worth noting. Do we want to change something in ourselves, or do we want to change someone/something in the environment? Is the change something specific or general, petty or cosmic in nature? This general sentence is often a good point of departure for discussion with ourselves and someone else concerning our feelings about what is blocking our world from developing and what our point of focus is in life.

13. This sentence rallies thoughts and feelings about current choices

and decision-making. Often it also surprises us that we are *not* entertaining any options now, and the difficulty in finishing the sentence is tied to our present conservatism and possible stagnation in life.

14. Nostalgia, remorsefulness, and a general contrast between our current situation/abilities and those of the past generally come up here.

15. Our image of God is tapped. Our positive and negative thoughts, as well as the manner and maturity of our images, are a source of exploration and reflection here.

16. This question on the Bible is general. It may indicate the amount of importance and attention we give the Sacred Scriptures (i.e., whether we even read the Bible on a regular basis), or point to some specific reaction regarding our reading of it.

17. A fear that we are ashamed of should surface here. Its etiology, current implications, and reasonableness in terms of our present situation may be explored.

18. By looking ahead to our death, we can gain a possible perspective on how we want to live our lives and what we really should see as important and be acting upon. Meditating on this question can aid in correcting styles of living that are tied to petty issues and fail to take into account larger, communal, deeper aspects of Christian life.

19. Needs surrounding the father figure in our lives may turn up here. General reflections about father ("My father rarely drank or smoked.") may also be noted. However, reflection on this sentence in terms of what we felt about what was missing in our relationship with our fathers can often be quite fruitful in determining possibly repressed needs surrounding our acceptance of or motivation by authority figures.

20. Feelings and thoughts about personal inadequacies and sensitivity about any possible lack of understanding and support on the part of others come up here. This is an important topic to discuss with a colleague or mentor. It centers on the image we have of ourselves and the one we believe we project to others. We are also helped to understand when we are making excuses for our behavior and when we are being seen unrealistically by others.

21. Seeing God in ourselves helps us reflect on the positive, personal presence of the Eternal Being. Too often we only reflect on our-

selves in order to deal with our own sinfulness and don't balance it by crediting the graceful presence of God in our own psychoreligious terrain. This is a good area to reflect on and discuss with a pastoral counselor, mentor, spiritual director, or retreat guide.

22. This question is in line with 4, 5, 8, and 12. It points to what we would do with power as well as to our frustrations about our own impotence. Our needs and feelings of injustice may also come to the fore in the way we finish this sentence and associate other thoughts to it.

23. This sentence centering on potential ability may elicit some guilt concerning efforts we have not made. It may also point to abilities we have, but have not been able to actualize because of a perceived lack of opportunity. A future plan about employing such untapped talents and possible additional frustrations in their utilization may be developed in reflecting on this sentence.

24. For women, images of their role models come out here. Feelings about ideals ("There's no such thing as an ideal woman. An ideal woman is my mother.") also come out. For those of us who are men, our image of women in contemporary society, our sexism, and our thoughts about our mothers may come out in this sentence.

25. This question is in line with past ones, but fits in particularly well with 11 and 12. Perceived problems in self and the environment, as well as the actions taken in the past and planned for the future to deal with them, usually come out of reflection on this completed sentence.

26. In keeping with 21, this sentence is designed to evaluate the mindset we have with respect to keeping ourselves open to God and the Christlike ministry we have as our responsibility each day.

27. This is a very open-ended sentence. Its extreme lack of structure provides an opportunity for the person to project thoughts and feelings which can open up a personal reflection or dialogue not dealt with sufficiently in other sentences.

28. This sentence is analogous to 24.

29. In line with 21 and 26, this question provides an opportunity for noting where we feel we are being led today by God. With a spiritual director or retreat leader, discussion of how we discern whether the message is coming from our needs or God's direction can be helpful.

30. An area that we consciously recognize as a block, but perhaps

unconsciously are getting secondary (indirect) gain out of, should come up here. Discussion with ourselves as to what we are gaining by maintaining what we recognize as unproductive behavior can aid in personal growth. For instance, we may be impulsive, but if we begin to recognize the "advantage" of acting immediately to gain closure, we may be able to stop the behavior by accepting the inner turmoil of postponing the gratification if we clearly, consciously note the reinforcement our impulsive action provides.

31. This sentence is in line with a previous one on writing our own epitaph. It speaks to goals and accomplishments as well.

32. Our present recognition of the creative continuing presence of God in us and our community is the focus in this sentence.

33. Guilt and its reasonableness can be unveiled here. Thought should be given as to *whether the guilt is temporary and facilitates action, or if it is a heavy permanent guilt that fires despair.* Specific sources of guilt can also be explored here. (This is a particularly good area to discuss with a director, counselor, or colleague.)

34. Reflection on self without attention to special talent(s) would be imbalanced. This sentence seeks to highlight our positives and start us on the road to accepting them. Some thought about our talents not being appreciated by others, or our not using them to the fullest, may come out too.

35. This sentence is a check on 29. We should check for consistency as well as how we felt about the question being asked again. (Do we become suspicius and wonder if we are not projecting ourselves as we feel others would have us?)

36. A general question on sex and our own sexuality. Vagueness in this area or negative or hesitant feelings or thoughts are especially worth following up in discussion with another key person whose opinions we value.

37. This sentence should be used to open a potential dialogue with ourselves (and a possibly "significant other") about what we consider to be our main liability. Thoughts about why this is such a problem and the steps we have already taken to deal with the problem can provide a basis for future plans of intervention.

38. This sentence is fairly straightforward in focus. However, if

there is no recent gift we can recognize from God, attention as to how we are closing the door to God's freely given grace may be helpful.

39. Feelings and thoughts about anger, as well as how we accept and handle anger in ourselves and others, should be included in reflection on this topic. Since dealing with anger is one of the most difficult processes for Christians, some time should be given to this area.

40. The nature of the desire, as well as the reason no one suspects or has been told about it, are the subject of revelation and examination here.

41. The source of embarrassment as well as the reason why this area is so disconcerting to the image we want to project should be of interest in looking at this sentence.

42. Relationship with father and authority and the implications for this are covered again here.

43. This complements our look at the present and the past with a view to "our future life and style of living with God." The question of mission should be discussed with respect to the way this sentence is completed.

44. This sentence addresses again the way we view our family and, in turn, how we feel about the way our needs were met.

45. Why we are sensitive, as well as *what* we are sensitive to, are the topics for exploration in this sentence completion.

46. What is the driving force behind us? When and how do we have the opportunity to become fully alive in this way? What do I do to put myself in the position of being fully alive? These are some of the questions addressed here.

47. An open question designed to offer us a platform for free association.

48. Another sentence completion designed to open up our discussion with regard to our relationship (or lack of it) with God.

49. A further validity check on what we have previously responded to with respect to mother and nurturance.

50. The question of prohibition and guilt are dealt with again here.

51. For the cleric or religious, this sentence will tap expectations about community living. Unrealistic expectations as well as reasonable

goals for community living will be noted. For those of us who are lay-persons, this topic will tap our interest in being part of the mystical body of Christ, or will point us in the necessary direction of being interested in the concept of community and the corporate aspect of salvation (the communion of saints).

52. How severe or lacking is our conscience (what the psychoanalytic literature calls the "superego")? How balanced is our moral fiber with our spontaneous impulses and desires? This sentence addresses these questions.

53. Another question on needs—this time a quite general and open one—is presented to stimulate us to think about this area.

54. Burnout can result in part from losing touch with our own religious life.. This partial sentence brings to light those efforts we make to bring the gospel to ourselves while we are reaching out to evangelize others. If we answer this inadequately, it may mean that we are setting ourselves up for an attack on our personal faith and confidence in God.

55. We say something about ourselves when we describe when and where we feel most comfortable, and under what circumstances we *don't* feel comfortable. This sentence taps these times and places and gives us the opportunity to think about the implications of this.

56. What makes us happy? Who is able to lift our spirits? What accomplishments bring us a sense of satisfaction? What setting brings us joyous peace? The answers to one or more of these questions and reflection upon them gives us an insight into our personalities, goals, and style of living.

57. This sentence explores our view of what constitutes a *total* commitment on *our* part to living the Christian life. It also provides the standard against which to review how we are doing now. If we choose to discuss this answer with another person, some feedback on the reality and extent of our goals and whether they are motivating us or threatening us by pointing to our lack of efforts would be helpful.

58. This is another look at our personal sensitivities and when they come into play.

59. Review of our experiences of closeness with God and what types of things bring us to this feeling are noted here. Some consideration of

the relationship of feelings to thought with respect to believing we are close to God would be helpful here (If we don't *feel* good after meditating or a period of prayer, does that mean we are not close to God?)

60. This open-ended partial sentence on "subtle sinfulness" is designed to elicit comments on our view of the nuances of sin in our lives and the lives of others.

61. What gets us down? How badly do we become depressed? What do we do about it? How effective are we in dealing with such periods? How do people react to us when we are down? Are we able to cope with our depressions? What methods do we use to deal with periods of serious sadness? Are we able to ask for help at these times? The list of questions we can ask in reflecting on our completion of this sentence can help us understand the etiology of the times we become somewhat depressed, and our method of coping with them.

62. How we feel about being in charge as well as our ability to be assertive (as opposed to aggressive or passive) can be examined in reviewing this sentence with ourselves and those with whom we feel free to talk about our lives.

63. Once again we view our connection with God by focusing on the ministry and life of Christ, the type of life we are living, and the attitude we have in approaching others in need.

64. The focus on the kind of person we get along with, or the revelation that we get along with only a few people or many types of individuals, provides helpful information in terms of what kind of person we are and our style of interpersonal relations. For instance, if we get along with only a few people, does that really mean we are very shy, fearful, sensitive, uncertain, or tentative? If we get along with *everybody*, is that good, or are we swallowing too much anger and avoiding standing on principle because we fear the anger of others? From the positive side, what are the kinds of things about us that make us attractive to others?

65. This sentence picks up on 64 and emphasizes why people like us. This completion is also designed to get us to look more closely at how nice we are without fearing we are being narcissistic. True humility demands that we be as courageous in looking at our talents and positive points as we are fearless in looking at our personal liabilities.

66. This is an open-ended question which looks at what we feel is missing in our lives now. It can open a discussion with ourselves as to how we have coped with such losses and what we are doing to move on in spite of them.

67. Present personal struggles are the subject of this sentence completion. This area should change from time to time, but it is important to see if there is a pattern to such struggles and whether there is an unproductive pattern to the way we have dealt with them over the years. Are the struggles now really new, or are they old issues in new clothing?

68. Laughter is good medicine and laughing at ourselves and our idiosyncracies can be quite healing. The times we take ourselves too seriously are those times when we may lose perspective. Such times as these should be touched upon in this sentence completion. Trying to uncover the reasons why we have a hard time moving away from defensiveness so we can laugh at ourselves could also be a goal of reflection here.

69. This mention of compulsion ties in with the previous questions on "being stubborn" and with those instances where others feel we can do something but *we* feel we really can't. Just as reinforcement schedules are at the basis of compulsions, new behaviors to undo them can be learned. Particularly if this response is discussed with a trusted helper, the reflection and subsequent actions taken with respect to this area may be beneficial.

70. When a person aggravates us, it means that the person is able to touch sensitive, vulnerable areas. In looking at the type of person (or the specific person) who bothers us the most, we need to look at why we are giving them that kind of power over our emotions. Even if what they are doing is inappropriate, the fact that they are getting such a disproportionate emotional rise out of us means that we have not fully resolved something within ourselves. Consequently, this sentence fits in nicely with the previous ones dealing with personal sensitivity and anger.

71. A look at areas of growth and possible atrophy of faith and styles of believing are the topics here. Our response should be compared with other ones we have completed in the same area (for instance, our image of God now).

72. This one addresses the same area as 69, but has more of a focus on *conscious* refusal rather than the feeling that we are being forced by something we don't have control over. We need to ask ourselves, "Why are we not willing to _____" as part of the reflection on this response. Sometimes we don't examine our stand because it has always seemed sound, but as time changes, sometimes previously sensible stands lose their current validity.

73. This stimulus asks us to look at our alcohol consumption. Why do we drink? How much? When? Are we drinking more now? Is it out of our control? Do we drink alone? Are we using alcohol more or less now? Why have our drinking patterns changed for the better or for the worse?

74. While this question is meant to elicit a response which would say something about ourselves by noting which passage from sacred scripture appeals to us most, it is also meant to encourage us to read the Bible with this question in mind.

75. Who was this person? When did we know him or her? What were we going through then? How did he or she make a difference? Is he or she still in our lives? Who is making an impact on our lives now? All of these questions can be addressed as part of the reflective discussion with ourselves concerning our response to this partial sentence.

6

Burnout and Commitment

The primary goal of Christian Introspection is to help us take care of ourselves pastorally so we can, in turn, undertake the necessary personal struggles which are part of being of real service to others. The more we understand ourselves and nurture our true needs, the stronger we can be for others amidst today's turmoil. The more we appreciate our own talents and lovable attributes, the greater will be our ability to use them for others. And finally, the more clearly we are able to see our own human tendencies to withdraw from life narcissistically or put our own unnecessary, unhealthy needs first, the better we will be able to curb such parochial self-centeredness.

In helping us to discern who we are and who we are becoming, Christian Introspection can also aid us to see when we are becoming over-involved and over-extended in our efforts to reach out to others. In being Christ-like, there is a danger of falling into a savior complex and trying to be all things to all people all of the time (i.e., be God!). If we fall into this trap, we are not only guilty from a theological point of view of the sin of pride, but, from a psychological perspective, we are also setting ourselves up for personal "burnout."

"Burnout" is a topic on many people's minds today. Much has been said about it in professional conferences, journals, and books, as well as in the news media and popular magazines. But this phenomenon is actually not new. Rather, it is a different, more comprehensive way of looking at how stress and depression can take their toll, especially on those who are committed to helping others. Certainly among this group we must include committed, involved lay and religious Christians, as is pointed out in the following statements by a minister and a priest on the topic:

Where does the fire go? Again and again, ministers burn out. They lose their enthusiasm and excitement; they become bored and pedantic; and they decide to leave the ministry and enter other occupations.

Burnout is a hazard common to the service professions . . . . But ministers are especially hard hit because there is a stigma attached to leaving the ministry. It's seen as a spiritual failure, and those who leave often suffer a special kind of guilt about failing to fulfill their call.

Fortunately, burnout is not inevitable. It's often tied to misconceptions about the nature of Christian ministry, reluctance to change traditional pastoral roles, and unrealistic idealism about a minister's humanity. Burnout doesn't have to happen. If forewarned of the dangers, ministers might better anticipate, plan for, and work through this threat.[1]

Why is it that activists in Jesuit social ministry seem to have the longevity of members of a bomb squad? Why is it that brevity seems to be the one common characteristic of a wide variety of forms of social ministry in direct contact with the poor and the problems of the poor? What the title expression "burn-out" refers to is a physical, emotional, psychological, and spiritual phenomenon—an experience of personal fatigue, alienation, failure *and more*—that seems characteristic of the lives of a number of Jesuit social activists in this country.[2]

The thought expressed above in both quotes is the threat of burnout for Christians who are *involved*—Christians who have not lost their recognition of Christ's cross and his life of ministry. Yet in making the witness, is such a quick, wounded martyrdom necessary?

Psychology and psychiatry have been actively responding to this question with theories and methods of intervention. In addition, an appreciation of some key theological and biblical aspects of hope have direct bearing on Christian commitment and burnout. So the topic of burnout is a good one for us to treat here. It illustrates a theme which integrates psychology and theology and is the kind of issue ideal for consideration in a book on the Christian Introspection process.

Psychology of Burnout

The word "burnout" dramatically describes the caring person whose reservoir of energy and motivation is presently depleted. The

burnout phenomenon has been noted as a serious problem in the helping professions: mental health, education, medicine, social work, and
religion. No one in these groups is immune. In religion, the Christian
volunteer, the committed family-life leader, the bishop, the religious
sister, the pastor, the deacon, the caring, morally conscious Christian
parent, the youth minister—all of us who are truly invested partici-
pants in the church—are potential candidates for burnout!

What Is Burnout?

Burnout is a psychological difficulty caused by perceived excessive
demands on a person, over a period of time, which results in a temporary or fairly permanent loss of energy, motivation, self-confidence,
and idealism. The reported symptoms and visible signs of burnout are
similar to ones seen in people under stress and those experiencing depression. The difference with burnout is that we see a combination of
symptoms and signs, and the person most prone to it is the sensitive
helper with a strong sense of purpose and commitment.

What Does Burnout Look Like?

Physically, the picture of burnout can be varied, but the words
"listless" and "uncomfortable" usually apply. There is a sense of general fatigue which in turn may lead to exhaustion. Even though the
person spends more time in bed, sleeplesness and restlessness prevent
the individual from achieving a rested feeling.

Frequent uncomfortable physical symptoms are also present. A
lingering cold, body aches, mild headaches, and upset stomachs are
some of the difficulties which arise to make life irritating and impos-
sible to deal with in a relaxed fashion.

Psychologically, the picture of burnout is that of a person who
seems as if he or she has been subjected to the pressures and indecen-
cies of the world. There is a sense that "if one more person says something to me, or I get one more assignment, I'll blow my top!" Also,
there is a sense of inefficiency: the motivated, organized approach to
life that once worked well seems gone. The person is now fatigued,
listless, and apathetic.

The following illustration demonstrates one way in which the above physical and psychological signs and symptoms manifest themselves. (In addition, we are given an indication of what type of person might be an ideal candidate for burnout, as well as some of the primary causes of this problem.)

I am a permanent deacon in the Catholic Church. I have been now for three years. About five years ago I was a leader in the charismatic movement and doing work with Marriage Encounter. I really felt fulfilled. I worked hard, saw results, and had great expectations for myself and the church. I was appreciated and felt I had a place where I could cheerfully grow. The next logical step was to develop my lay apostolate a step further. I felt that I could be of more use as a bridge between the laity and the priests, sisters, and brothers by being ordained as a permanent deacon. It would give me the best of both worlds, so to speak. Instead it left me in limbo and caused me nothing but trouble.

Unlike the other movements I had been involved in, the people in the parish didn't seem to want to participate. We'd set up a meeting and two people would show; in the past, if it were a Marriage Encounter we'd pack them in. Also, in the charismatic movement I was accepted. I thought I would have more status as a permanent deacon and do more good; instead some of the parishoners—and priests for that matter—seemed to resent me.

Even when I planned a program that did come off well, the work was frustrating because I constantly had to check everything ten times with the pastor. Also, he would decide something about the program, and if it didn't go well, I would be left holding the bag for it.

Slowly but surely it started taking its toll. Now I feel like I'm moving in slow motion. I'm more and more tired after the week is over, but I'm not accomplishing nearly as much. Maybe it's because I feel so terrible; my neck seems stiff, my sinuses are driving me crazy this year, and I can't remember the last time I slept through the night.

Candidates and Causes

The above illustration of the permanent deacon may prompt one to conclude rightly that *powerlessness, lack of appreciation,* and *ambiguity in role* all contribute to setting the stage for burnout. Yet candidates for burnout need not be ones who have new roles or ones that lack an element of authority. This is pointed out in the following statement by Norbert Brockman from his article on burnout in superiors:

When a superior finds himself sitting at his desk, not resting, but just not able to go through the day's mail or to handle even one little problem, he is experiencing burnout. The advisor who dreads a chapter or a council meeting, and through it keeps counting the time until it's over, is experiencing burnout. The formation person who finds himself planning a series for his candidates, less because of how it will enhance the formation program and more because "someone else" will give it and *he* doesn't have to be present, is experiencing burnout.[3]

Consequently, the committed Christian regardless of ecclesiastical position can be a candidate for burnout. By reviewing the work of those professionals who have studied and written on the problem, it is possible to develop a partial list of the types of Christians who have a greater chance of experiencing more serious forms of burnout. (see Figure 2).

As we review the list, further insight into the causes of burnout is possible. As we can see (figure 3), the reasons or contributing factors to burnout are also quite numerous and varied, so a strategy for prevention and intervention is necessary if we are to remain committed without unnecessarily losing our fervor in the process.

Figure 2

Christian Candidates for Burnout

---

1. Undisciplined Christian activists.
2. Persons constantly involved in an intense helping role.
3. Helpers with a vague or poorly understood role.
4. People who are continually being depended upon, but who themselves are not able to take—or feel guilty about taking—time off for personal physical, psychological, and spiritual replenishment.
5. Persons who have multiple (sometimes conflicting) role expectations and/or responsibility for too many individuals without the assistance of other helpers.
6. Extremely perfectionistic individuals (especially those in positions where the structure is weak and there is a strong requirement to be flexible and patient in dealing with the situations that come up each day).

7. Persons who are in demanding people-oriented activities but who lack a growthful prayer life.
8. Helpers in complex human settings who lack the training, supervision, or continuing education to develop professionally and gain perspective on the situation.

Figure 3

Causes for Burnout Among Committed Christians

---

1. Inadequate time for prayer, physical rest, cultural diversion, further education, and personal psychological replenishment.
2. Vague criteria for success and/or inadequate positive feedback on efforts made.
3. Guilt over failures, and over taking out time to nurture oneself properly and deal with one's own legitimate needs.
4. Unrealistic ideals that are threatening rather than generally motivating.
5. Inability to deal with anger.
6. Extreme need to be liked by others, prompting unrealistic involvement with others.
7. Neglect of emotional, physical, and spiritual health.
8. Poor community life and/or unrealistic expectations and needs surrounding the support and love of others for us.
9. Working with people (peers, superiors, those coming for help) who are burned out.
10. Extreme powerlessness to effect needed change or being overwhelmed by paperwork or administrative tasks.
11. A serious lack of appreciation by our superiors, colleagues, or those whom we are trying to serve.
12. Sexism, ageism, racism, or other prejudice experienced directly in our lives and work.
13. High conflict in the family, home, work, or living environment.

14. A serious lack of charity among those with whom we must live or work.
15. Extreme change during times in life when maturational crises and adjustment are also occurring (for example, 48-year-old female religious who is being asked to work with difficult adolescent youths at a time when she is experiencing conflict over growing older and thinks she has lost some of her physical attractiveness).
16. Seeing money wasted on projects that seem to have no relation to helping people or Christian activism.
17. Not having the freedom or power to deal with or absent oneself from regularly occurring stressful events.
18. A failure to curb one's immature reasons for helping others and to develop more mature ones in the process.
19. The "savior complex"—an inability to recognize what we can and cannot do in helping others in need.
20. Overstimulation, or isolation and alienation.

Prevention and Intervention

Since the literature on stress, depression, and burnout is immense, trying to capture fully the depth of the findings on prevention and treatment here is unrealistic. However, there are four words that may suggest ways to avoid the unnecessary stress or pressure in our lives that lead to burnout. They are: balance, expectations, knowledge, and support.

Balance has already been treated in chapter 3. Yet it is so important it merits re-emphasis here. We need to examine ourselves carefully to determine what the ideal balance is for us between the various polarities in life. (In leadership roles we need to also be wary of projecting our styles and weighted balances on others. Some of us are action oriented, others move at a more measured pace; neither need be incorrect, just unique.) When there is an imbalance, we need to ask why, and whether it is temporary. Not to find out whether our life is getting out of hand without taking responsibility for setting it back on course can be problematic.

For instance, if we are working long hours with demanding tasks, while play and prayer have practically disappeared from our lives, we need to search out the source of the imbalance by asking ourselves a number of questions:

Is this lack of physical and psychospiritual energy and motivation something temporary, or have I set myself up for burnout?

What is the value of personal meditation and "holiday hours" (coffee breaks, evenings with friends) in my life?

Do I feel guilty about replenishing myself physically and emotionally? If so, why?

Has something changed in my life that makes me feel that I *need* to work so hard that I'm neglecting myself? (Am I trying to prove something to someone or to myself?)

What kind of positive and negative feedback am I getting from the environment because I'm working so hard? (Are people telling me not to work so hard, but indirectly giving me signs that they expect me to labor continuously?)

This type of questioning in the Christian Introspection mode is important in order to uncover the sources and ramifications of imbalances in our lives so they can be corrected.

Expectations can also be a source of burnout when they are unrealistic. We need to assess continually whether our personal expectations or the ones we have of others are a source of inspiration or represent a threat or source of disappointment. Questions such as the following need to be asked:

How much do I expect to be appreciated for what I do?

Do I expect everyone to like me and respect me?

Does what I expect of myself turn out to be a source of motivation for me to be the best I can, or a source of personal disappointment? ("I'm not as good as I should be; I'm failing in my vocation.")

Are my expectations of others tied to the reality of the situation or based on my own unresolved needs to be loved? ("Do I serve others so they will like me and tell me how great I am, or primarily because I want to be of service?")

Knowledge is also essential to prevent or terminate the tendency toward burnout. This knowledge is knowledge of self, awareness of others, and an understanding of the psychology of ministry. If we don't know ourselves, seek to recognize what others are experiencing and who they are at this point in life, and try to appreciate the complexity in ministering to others (family, friends, colleagues, those in need of assistance, etc.), burnout is almost inevitable.

If we don't know ourselves, we stumble around blindly merely hoping we will get our needs met without any awareness of what they are and whether they are realistic. If we don't seek to appreciate the psychological and spiritual place others are coming from, we may interact with them in a way that lacks sensitivity and reciprocity. If we don't try to employ basic principles in counseling and helping others, we are running the risk of becoming too involved and pulled down by others or—at the other end of the spectrum—unnecessarily fearful of being with someone in a time of need because we are afraid we are going to "say the wrong thing." So, in keeping with the word knowledge, some of the types of questions we should be asking ourselves include:

How do I perceive my current work and living situations? Are they supportive? If so, when are they? If not, what is contributing to this?

Do I feel I am making the most of my current situation? How am I doing this and how am I failing in this regard?

When something unpleasant happens, do I analyze the situation to see what part I played in making the situation better or worse?

How do I learn from stress and rejection? (Do I seek to understand myself and others better when things don't go my way to see how I might benefit from such knowledge?)

What are my realistic and immature motivations to help specific people in my life whom I am in the process of supporting emotionally?

Do I really try to be empathic with others so I am not surprised by their expectations and demands of me?

How do I work to continue to develop my knowledge of professional issues in psychology and theology?

Support certainly goes hand in hand with knowledge and the other two key areas for reflection in our efforts to prevent and curb burnout.

Without the feeling that others love us and support us, life becomes more difficult than it need be. In looking to our relationship with God for sustenance, we must also look for God in the community we have with others. Our love for them and their love for us brings God to life in our lives *now*. Too little support can bring on alienation and the feeling we are all alone and cut off. If we cut ourselves off then we are islands which can be swamped by the pains of living much more easily than if we link ourselves with others.

Some of us have not bothered to seek out others because we fear rejection. Others, who have had a paucity of love in childhood, seek to use others to fill our almost insatiable need for affection. By asking ourselves questions in this area we can increase our awareness of the importance of support, the most reasonable way to get it, realistic sacrifices we can make for it, and when our needs get in the way of our having satisfying interpersonal relationships. Here are some questions we might ponder:

What kinds of people do we seek out as friends and why?

Are we willing to entertain relationships with different types of people?

Are we frightened of being clear with people about our personal feelings because we are afraid to lose them as friends?

Do we share too much with others too quickly, or do we fail to share enough but then expect others to be open with us?

Are we clear about our own values in life, and can we share them without trying to force them on others?

When we are angry, do we own up to the anger and try to see what is happening in interpersonal encounters to bring it on?

What do we expect of our community, friends, and family? Do we expect too much, or have we failed to become involved with others in our life?

Can we reach out to others when we are feeling down and anxious? Are we constantly complaining and crying to others?

Do we feel that we are a member of a group, or are we becoming more and more alienated from the natural communities of people with whom we should be involved (a spiritual director, more experienced colleagues, etc.)?

Have we found supportive supervisors in our lives who can help us in time of need?

Do we find we can express our feelings clearly and often enough without burdening others or making them feel that it is always their fault we are suffering?

In being honest with others, do we also remember we should be charitable too and get the same type of respect from them?

These questions regarding support point to the relative importance this area has in the prevention of burnout. If we have love, and are able to share it and receive it from others, we can undergo much stress. If we feel alone and unsupported, we can soon become easily crushed by the buffeting which comes with an active Christian life. When we feel the ability to be open, warm, relaxed, honest, and clear with others, renewal and growth are possible even when times are hard. Similarly, when others can be that way with us without fear of being hurt or abandoned, we give them a gift of special value; whether we reflect on the realities of our own lives, or the literature on burnout, this point should be easy for all of us to support.

The Role of a Theology of Hope in the Life of an Active, Committed Christian

Much of the burnout literature, even the material published in Christian publications, points to information which is helpful from the fields of psychology and psychiatry. However, in terms of avoiding burnout while avoiding the other extreme (avoiding Christian involvement as a reaction to being hurt from working with people in need), the help that a sound theology of hope can play is not always clearly noted.

A contemporary, challenging theology of hope can provide us with a christologically-based orientation which can help us gain perspective in life and avoid burnout. Yet it doesn't have to be one which provides instant release from the pain of the "now" of existence. On the contrary, it may offer us more pain—the pain of knowing we are responsible to and for others, the pain of yearning and groaning for the coming of the Kingdom of God (Romans 8:21).

Such a theology of hope would then militate against "privatism." Unlike some popular eschatological literature (e.g., Hal Lindsey's *The Late Great Planet Earth*), which denies the cross and ministry of Christ and instead claims that Christians don't have to worry about the world community but should just want to be saved, such a theology demands a greater emphasis on solidarity with the world.

Daniel Migliore points to this in his book *Called to Freedom: Liberation Theology and the Future of Christian Doctrine*. In his work we see how hope and community go together when we are speaking of a hope grounded in Jesus Christ.

> Jesus liberates us for friendship and solidarity with others, especially with the despised and the oppressed. This confession is more than a memory and more than a present experience. It is a world-encompassing hope . . . .
> What would be the features of a community today that lived in the power of this Spirit of freedom and within the horizon of this hope?
> 1. A Spirit-filled community would be an inclusive community . . .
> 2. A Spirit-filled community would be a community that does not try to evade experiences of suffering and negation . . .
> 3. A Spirit-filled community would be a community that celebrates the liberating grace of God here and now. As Paul instructed, it would rejoice greatly because the Lord is at hand (Phil. 4:4–5).[4]

Here we can see the influence of Jürgen Moltmann, whose extensive work on the theology of hope also supports an embrace of our living responsibilities. As he views it, we must see all statements about the future grounded in the history of Jesus Christ. In this way we distinguish the "spirit of eschatology" from the "spirit of utopia."

The "spirit of utopia" comes about when hope for the future is *not* grounded in the person and history of Jesus Christ, but in ourselves. We begin to have grandiose expectations of ourselves and the social revolutions or changes we hope to implement. With such an unrealistic hope, we then proceed until we burn out.

In the "spirit of eschatology" we avoid an *undisciplined* activism based primarily on a belief in our own abilities and the talents of the world. Instead, we have faith in God's promises, and being mindful of Christ's life, death, *and resurrection*, we struggle against the present injustices of the world as Christ did, with an eye to God's ultimate intervention.

So in line with Moltmann's work on Christian eschatology, we need to recognize the importance of founding our hope on Christ rather than on something (one) else. Likewise in doing this, we need to avoid moving into an extremist position (e.g. the dangers of "over faith"—passively sitting by without bearing necessary suffering as we wait for God to come and sweep us up to heaven on a cloud—or, "hope without faith" —depending only upon ourselves and our movements (socialist, capitalist, Marxist) rather than Jesus Christ who is God).

According to Moltmann then,

> Hope is nothing else than the expectation of those things which faith has believed to have been truly promised by God. In the Christian life faith has the priority, but hope the primacy. Without faith's knowledge of Christ, hope becomes a utopia and remains hanging in the air. But without hope, faith falls to pieces, becomes a fainthearted and ultimately a dead faith. . . . Those who hope in Christ can no longer put up with reality as it is, but begin to suffer under it, to contradict* it. Peace with God means conflict with the world, for the goal of the promised future stabs inexorably into the flesh of every unfulfilled present.[5]

So to Jürgen Moltmann, true hope—hope founded in the life, death, and resurrection of Jesus Christ—is a painful healer. It does not bring us above the world, but instead brings us to it in witness. So while it does offer the joy of a knowledge of God being faithful to his promises in the past and the present, we are forced to toil amidst a world marked by sin.

Once again, in Moltmann's words:

> Love does not snatch us from the pain of time, but takes the pain of the temporal upon itself. Hope makes us ready to bear the "cross of the present." It can hold to what is dead, and hope for the unexpected. It can approve of movement and be glad of history.[6]

---

*"Contradict" here means "fight against, struggle against."

We need this openness to "movement" and "the unexpected." Otherwise new, necessary challenges will be set aside in favor of a mentality of retrenchment. Without a cosmic Christian hope, our faith and love will then become an intramural activity rather than a Christian struggle for the salvation of the *whole* created order. The theme of hope, then, can help us avoid stagnation and selfism. We can become attuned to the cost of discipleship that Dietrich Bonhoeffer (the German theologian martyred by the Nazis) noted in his writings on the subject. Even in our meditations and reflections, we can keep hope alive in a way that demonstrates Christian Introspection, rather than preoccupied self-analysis.

Gustavo Gutiérrez, a prominent liberation theologian, also saw this, and Migliore points to it in his emphasis on the need for a spirituality of liberation.

> We need a spirituality that frees us to work for the development of very different social attitudes and practices. We need a spirituality that connects us with the groaning of the whole creation for freedom. Gutiérrez is surely right: we need not less interest in the spiritual life but a radical transformation of it. We need a new spirituality that is inclusive rather than exclusive, active as well as receptive, oriented to the coming of God's kingdom of righteousness and freedom throughout the world. We need a spirituality of liberation that will open us increasingly to a life of solidarity with others, especially the poor.[7]

When we view Moltmann's theology of hope, we can see how it and liberation theology are interwoven. We can see how the use of such a theme in the reflective process can urge the Christian to be Christlike, to recognize that while Christian hope is resurrection hope, it is also tied to the cross and ministry of Jesus. Yet though we can now see how the theme of hope can prevent extreme "privatism" and self-interest, we are now still left with some question as to how an awareness of one's theology of hope can also help in the prevention of burnout.

Theology of Hope and Unnecessary Martyrdom

In keeping with the connection of Christian self-awareness and personal involvement, more and more works are coming out in support of the need for reflective periods for social activists. One such creative collection is *The Wind Is Rising: Prayer Ways for Active People* published by the Quixote Center in Maryland. One paper is particularly relevant; it is titled "Noisy Contemplation."

> The Church is calling us to a more involved way of following Christ. We are being summoned to preach the Good News to a world in need of healing. Deep prayer and contemplation are needed to nurture, sustain, and integrate our lives. This prayer must be able to grow and flourish on the noise of our involved lives. Fragmented family life, transient life styles, rapid changes and high levels of tension make traditional forms of prayer difficult today, or available only to a few resourceful people. A new kind of deep prayer is needed for ordinary people.
> The dream is not to pray once in a while, or for a regular interval each day. Instead, we dream of praying throughout our daily lives. Such a life of prayer welcomes times apart to bring perspective and relief. But our prayer is not limited to such moments. Jesus showed us a life in which the bulk of his praying was done in the very midst of an active, involved life.[8]

This noisy contemplation, as it is called, surely should include the theme of hope. Just as a committed life is an active, prayerful life, hope can be an energetic force which helps bring perspective to the Christian's attitude and style of thinking.

Moltmann addresses this theme after discussing the reality of the present crosses Christians must and should bear in response to a theology of hope not merely tied to the rapture of the resurrection, but also to the other aspects of Christ's existence.

> Does this hope cheat man of the happiness of the present? How could it do so! For it is itself the happiness of the present. It pronounces the poor blessed, receives the weary and heavy laden, the humbled and wronged, the hungry and dying, because it perceives the

parousia of the kingdom for them. Expectation makes life good, for in expectation man can accept his whole present and find joy not only in its joy but also in its sorrow, happiness not only in its happiness but also in its pain. Thus hope goes on its way through the midst of happiness and pain, because in the promises of God it can see a future also for the transient, the dying and the dead.[9]

Thus with a theology of hope that has as its *ground* the vindication of God's promises to us in the resurrection of Jesus; has as its *object* the universality of the scope of redemption; and has as its *subject* the dualism of this age and the age to come, we can face today's world with some understanding and logic. With an ethics tied to both the Kingdom of God and Christ, we don't stand quietly staring into the heavens (Acts 1:10ff.). Nor do we feel that we alone have the future of the world in our hands. But with confidence in God we help to establish "beachheads" of the Kingdom of God looking to the salvation of the whole created order.

John F. Kennedy used to tell a story that bears repeating here:

Frank O'Connor, the Irish author, tells in one of his books how as a boy, he and his friends would make their way across the countryside and when they came to an orchard wall that seemed too high and too doubtful to try, and too difficult to permit their voyage to continue, they took off their hats and tossed them over the wall—and then they had no choice but to follow them.

With a sound theology of hope and appreciation of the psychology of burnout, high motivation to be of service to others is possible. Doubt and hesitation can fade, and commitment to working for Christ now need not end in disaster if we keep this in mind.

NOTES

1. H. Newton Maloney and Donald Falkenberg, "Ministerial Burnout," *Leadership* 1, no. 1 (1980), p. 57.

2. Alfred Krammer, "Burnout—Contemporary Dilemma for the Social Activist," *Studies in the Spirituality of Jesuits* 10, no. 1 (1978), p. 1.

3. Norbert Brockman, "Burnout in Superiors," *Review for Religious* 37 (1978), p. 809.

4. Daniel Migliore, *Called to Freedom: Liberation Theology and the Future of Christian Doctrine* (Philadelphia: Westminster, 1980), pp. 57–59.

5. Jürgen Moltmann, *Theology of Hope* (New York: Harper and Row, 1967), pp. 20, 21.

6. Ibid., p. 31.

7. Migliore, p. 89.

8. William Callahan, "Noisy Contemplation," in *The Wind is Rising: Prayer Ways for Active People*, edited by William Callahan and Francine Cardman (Mt. Ranier, Md.: Quixote Center, 1978), p. 37.

9. Moltmann, p. 32.

The Mystery Continues:
Some Final Comments on Christian Introspection

Christian Introspection *searches* to find out who we are and who we are in the process of becoming, *in light of the presence of the Spirit of God.* Though the process begins with the employment of psychological principles with us at the focus, the process doesn't end there. The search continually moves beyond us to God and others as we seek to gain a better understanding of what it means to be a Christian today and what challenges might be an outgrowth of our stance tomorrow.

As we search and counsel ourselves pastorally, the goal is not the avoidance of necessary pain. It is not a deification of self. It is not an abrogation of the responsibility to serve and be interested in others. Rather, it is a search to see how we can be strengthened and comforted by God in our goal to make life meaningful for ourselves and others. In this sense, only *unnecessary* masochistic pain is avoided; the suffering that comes with living a life full of the Spirit is accepted.

Our love of God, ourselves, and others is inextricably tied to our purpose, our "why" in life. The oft-mentioned quote "He who has a why for living can bear with almost any how" points to the importance of understanding our philosophy of life and personal talents. In appreciating this point, we recognize that we must continually search for our "why." We must never stop examining our own interior psychoreligious terrain. Self-identity is not achieved once and for all—

instead, we continually approach it through a sensitive openness to today's and tomorrow's new Spirit-filled opportunities to know and act.

As we grow in self-knowledge, we are able to give more. As we give more we can then help others to see for themselves how they can also give more. And when we enlarge our universe like this, the cosmos becomes greater for everyone we touch. As we touch them, they subsequently help us to greet Christ more openly. In Erich Fromm's words:

> You give joy, interest,
> understanding, knowledge, humor—
>   all that is alive in you.
> And by thus enhancing another's
>   sense of aliveness, you
> enhance your own.

There is no gimmicky way to do this. No prescribed path can be copied to discern where Christ is leading us. Today we often fail to see the value of life's simplicity. We begin to lose sight of the goals and Spirit of living and start to become so technique-oriented we forget our original purpose.

> A small businessman from the old country kept his accounts payable in a cigar box, his accounts receivable on a spindle, and his cash in the cash register. "I don't see how you can run your business this way," said his son. "How do you know what your profits are?"
>
> "Son," replied the businessman, "when I got off the boat, I had only the pants I was wearing. Today your sister is an art teacher, your brother is a doctor, and you're an accountant. I have a car, a home, and a good business. Everything is paid for. So you add it all up, subtract the pants, and there's your profit."

In this light, Christian Introspection is not meant to be a set of rules *guaranteed* to increase psychospiritual growth. Nor is it a compulsive attempt to capture the Holy Spirit in our lives. An obvious reality is: *We can't merit grace.* As William Stringfellow in his book *Count It All Joy* notes:

No matter how terrible the emptiness men endure within themselves and the alienation men suffer from all other men and all things in their estrangement from God, that does not blot out the gift. Or, to put it in the images of Genesis, after the Fall, in the depths of man's own life, the first characterization of God's response to rejection is of God walking in the garden calling to man "Where are you?" (Genesis 3:8–9). In sin men hide from God and conceal themselves from one another and fear even to behold themselves; but in the midst of that, God is seeking men.[1]

Christian Introspection does recognize, though, the need to seek to be virtuous. This need is closely connected with our responsibility to use what knowledge we have to move closer to God. This movement can take many shapes. The shape it takes in Christian Introspection is the removal of unnecessary defenses in our personality so we can provide a positive internal context to help us to be more Christ-like to others. We desire to remove the psychological blinders from our eyes. The goal, then, is *clarity*. The belief is: Clarity can bring us closer to God, closer to others . . . and fill us with a sense of the personal interior closeness we call *wholeness*.

NOTES

1. William Stringfellow, *Count It All Joy* (Grand Rapids, Michigan: Eerdmans, 1967), pp. 26–27.

Appendix 1
Common Questions About Christian Introspection

When lecturing and participating in small-group discussions or workshops on Christian Introspection, I am asked a number of common questions about the topic. A sampling of them appears below. In some instances the material presented is a review of the concepts, techniques, and issues discussed in earlier chapters. Other answers contain information which complements, or builds upon, the material presented thus far.

Is Christian Introspection intended for use by everyone or by a certain select group of Christian leaders?

Christian Introspection is clearly not intended for everyone. Since the process requires motivation, intelligence, and a degree of maturity, it is primarily designed for use by the adult Christian who is willing to expend the time and energy necessary to become involved in a structured, continuous self-examination in light of the death, resurrection, and ministry of Jesus Christ.

In addition to this general audience, the following types of groups have a natural interest in and opportunity to employ the Christian Introspection process:
1. Retreat directors and persons on retreat
2. Formation candidates and their directors
3. Divinity and pastoral-counseling students
4. Persons seeking growth in pastoral counseling
5. Parish discussion groups
6. Laity/religious in helping roles (teachers, guidance counselors, nurses, permanent deacons, directors/coordinators of religious education, family life/marriage encounter/charismatic leaders)

Since many of our motives and defenses against growth are unconscious (beyond our level of awareness), is self-analysis really worth the effort?

Self-analysis, in itself, will not uncover all our unconscious motives, and we should not expect to effect dramatic personality change by encountering our own styles of dealing with the world. Sigmund Freud, as a result of his own self-analysis, and Karen Horney, in her book on the subject, recognize and note the limitations of such a process. (It certainly can't substitute, for instance, for a process of psychotherapy or counseling.) However, with diligence and honesty, we can learn important information about ourselves through self-analysis.

So, although we shouldn't have unrealistic expectations about Christian Introspection, we should recognize that it does offer us great possibilities in its structured way of viewing conscious trends in our lives. Furthermore, by being so actively self-aware, we can also be honestly attuned to those "slips of the unconscious" that appear when we least expect them; and this is a potential source of deeper self-knowledge.

Isn't a little bit of knowledge a dangerous thing? By thinking we know ourselves aren't we setting ourselves up for the illusion that we have real self-knowledge?

Christian Introspection is not setting us up to be "armchair analysts"; rather it is putting in motion the responsibility we have to God, our neighbors, and ourselves to know as much about ourselves as we can. The alternative to searching out our motives and styles of Christian living is childish ignorance. We have a responsibility to look at ourselves and our lives as honestly as possible, with the true humility that what we perceive may not be as accurate as we think it is.

Somehow I feel that Christian Introspection is self-indulgent and cuts me off from the community God wants me to be part of in life. Are you saying we should put self ahead of community and that we should seek our own individual salvation and not worry about the corporate one?

Christian Introspection is *not* designed to cut us off from the community of God. Instead, by knowing ourselves and our human weaknesses and tendencies to seek personal salvation, as well as recognizing what talents we do have to offer, it offers us a chance to become a more useful, integral part of the community. Without self-awareness we stumble along and sometimes lose our place in the world. Christian Introspection can help us avoid "privatism" and individual pietism on the one hand, and undisciplined activism which can lead to burnout (and ultimate separation from the community) on the other. Knowing ourselves and being wrapped up in ourselves are two different things.

In Christian Introspection, is there an opportunity to involve another person(s) in the process?

Involving a retreat director, trusted peer or colleague, spiritual director, pastoral counselor, or someone who is generally involved in ministry to us can be *very* helpful. Such feedback not only helps us be more objective in analyzing thought-provoking themes, but is also ties us further to the Christian community of which we should be an active part.

How much time does Christian Introspection take?

There is no set amount of time that is prescribed. However, initially it should take an hour or two to fill out the Christian Introspection Sentence Completion Form. Following that, given the points provided in this book, we should count on spending at least fifteen minutes per day on reflection. More time than this would be helpful, but consistency is even more important.

In a nutshell, what would you say the steps of the Christian Introspection process are?

There are two phases. First, completion of and reflection on the Christian Introspection Sentence Completion Form should help us to begin uncovering and examining a broad array of life's issues. Second, we should set out a time each day to interview ourselves and write down—if possible—our thoughts, feelings, and associations according to the principles and techniques noted in this book. An optional third step is to share our reflections with someone we can trust and who can fill a position of ministry to us.

While looking at the essential steps, we should also try to remember the basic purpose of Christian Introspection: *to use principles of psychology in structured self-review so as to remove the blocks to God's movement in our lives.*

How necessary is it to write down our thoughts and reflections other than with respect to the Christian Introspection Form?

If writing down our thoughts and feelings become a block that prevents undertaking the Christian Introspection process, then we should not bother doing it. However, writing down our feelings, thoughts, and associations provides us with a record to check back on in the future. Such a diary of impressions can be very, very useful.

Is Christian Introspection as a one-time experience worth anything?

Yes, it is. People will often go to a minister, counselor, or professional helper for a one-time consultation. They will not go into a period of ongoing counseling or therapy, but get information that will help them break the log jam of life. Likewise, we might not feel ready to undertake an ongoing process of Christian Introspection. By using the Christian Introspection Sentence Completion Form we can bring out a number of factors that might have been eluding us. We might uncover talents, or we might see more clearly personal fears or anxieties that we had previously avoided. In retreats or the vocational discernment process, Christian Introspection can be a helpful springboard to the facilitation of self-awareness.

What if I find out that Christian Introspection is making me feel worse? Am I doing something wrong?

Self-understanding is not the same as self-indictment. There are times when certain knowledge and honesty with ourselves does make us temporarily sad or lead to realistic guilt. However, if the process of looking at ourselves in light of the gospels becomes a consistently self-deflating process it should be discontinued and employed only with the support of a counselor or therapist.

Is there anyone who should NOT employ the process of Christian Introspection?

Since the process involves a degree of intellectual and personal maturity, the process is *not* advised for someone who isn't an adult, or who is having notable emotional problems. Also, someone in counseling or therapy should consult with the person providing treatment as to the advisability of undertaking Christian Introspection. (Note: In pastoral counseling the helper may find the process an ideal way of *increasing* the growth rate and impact of the sessions with certain clients or patients.)

What is the difference between Christian Introspection and personal prayer?

Personal prayer focuses broadly on our relationship with God. We reach out to God and sometimes—in contemplation—intellectually or emotionally *experience* God. In Christian Introspection there is overlap with prayer, but the focus is narrower; as such, it is a supplement to prayer. The focus of Christian Introspection is our personality in terms of how this psychoreligious terrain reveals our God-given talents and our own sinful liabilities. We look at our relationship with ourselves and the world with an eye to the influence of God in our lives—"Who are we now and who are we becoming with respect to what God wants of us?" As we become healthier through Christian Introspection, our religious commitment and prayer life should develop as well, but Christian Introspection is never a substitute for prayer, just as therapy and pastoral counseling are never substitutes for spiritual direction.

Will Christian Introspection help me gain peace in these times of violence, economic chaos, and disregard for morality?

Christian Introspection may help you gain a sense of perspective and put you in a state I refer to as "peaceful pain," but it is not designed to allow you to rise above the world. We can gain relief by recognizing God's forgiveness and love of us. We can gain a sense of tranquility from an acceptance of ourselves and others. Through Christian Introspection we can seek and find love in the world, but it will not and should not make us impervious to the injustice and suffering that we must all fight and be chained under until the full coming of the Kingdom of God. Ironically, Christian Introspection may appear to be a way out of the world by going into ourselves. Instead it is, in fact, a deeper journey into the world as we honestly and responsibly search for God's continual call to community service.

Appendix 2
Christian Introspection Touchstones

This appendix consists of a brief collection of statements and questions on issues and themes which may encourage the reflective process. These quotes are to be used in conjunction with the review of passages from the Bible and theological works. By employing them in this manner they may help to integrate self-understanding with the much-needed recognition of what our community responsibilities are. Similarly, they may help us find the balance between the hopefulness of the gospel message and the conflicts of life which each Christian must embrace.

The pace of reviewing them will no doubt vary depending upon our current needs and concerns. Though this section can be skimmed through quickly, because of its stated purpose to facilitate a form of self-understanding which is in line with our call to discipleship we should pace ourselves so we can gain the most from the points presented.

These thoughts are merely points of departure. Ideally, some will facilitate thematic periods of Christian Introspection. Naturally, every point will not seem equally pertinent or applicable. It will depend upon individual, current needs. So, rereading them at different times during different affectual states (sad, happy, worried, joyful, agitated) is encouraged.

With this section as a possible model, each of us is then asked to begin developing a personal set of "touchstones." Personal reflections and quotes from theological, philosophical, and psychological works, as well as from other important sources (even novels which carry a message) which seem challenging, inspiring, enlightening, and supportive, should be recorded for further reflection. Also, the associations with them should be noted so that they can be shared with others (a close colleague, pastoral counselor, spiritual director, ministry representative) so a somewhat more objective response and further link with the Christian community is possible.

All of these steps take work. Yet if we are to lead a life of reflective discipleship, the effort must be made. Certainly the potential results of such an investment of time and energy would include the attainment of a better sense of direction in life. Any time we can bring together the knowledge of who we are with what Christ seems to be calling us to be and do in life *now*, there is a sense of clarity which sustains us even at times of extreme psychological and physical pain. This sense of "peaceful pain" is the greatest gift we can receive in a world that yearns for the final coming of the Kingdom of God.

Touchstones

It's hard to have vision if we're holding onto the present and still preoccupied with the past.

When I have clarity, I feel closest to God.

Actual humility means accepting the true extent of our negative self so that denial and avoidance can subside, thus allowing what is lovable about us to come through and be embraced with a sense of peaceful strength.

When we have hope, our goals inspire us; when we don't, they threaten us.

Each day the plan of life I used yesterday is outmoded. To forget this is to deny the vitality of the pilgrim church and to begin the idolatrous worship of a personal church molded by us instead of Christ.

Learning is having fun with the seriousness of knowledge. Learning about ourselves is enjoying the important gifts God has given to us.

All of us have good memories that *don't* serve us well; today's interpersonal needs are not appropriately fed by *yesterday's* styles of interaction, but often we act as if they are.

As passive resignation moves to active acceptance, healing begins.

Our islands of ideas and thoughts can be connected into differently shaped chains depending upon our motivations and mood. If we come to our thoughts without love, then self-indictment, self-pity, and extreme self-involvement will occur. Whereas if we reflect with a sense of love, self-understanding, openness to God and others, and renewal can result.

Christian Introspection is not meant to be a subject to be passed or failed with the grade of A or F. It is merely taking the time to glimpse the flashes of Light we need for the process of Christian journeying.

Being a frightened architect who doesn't work with the *living* blueprint God has given us in Christ can be just as bad as being a pompous architect who totally disregards the Christian plan for salvation we have been given for guidance.

Thinking or doing things that are generally out of character for us, or are not in line with our basic style of dealing with the world, should not be dismissed as irrelevant exceptions brought on by unusual circumstances. Instead they are hints of hidden elements. With them we need to seek a *creative synthesis* in understanding ourselves or we will be dismissing buried treasure which is of great potential psychoreligious value.

If we open the door to new ideas about ourselves, the winds which sweep them in may sometimes be unpleasantly hot or cold and leave us temporarily embarrassed or emotionally blue. However, if we remember the need we have to embrace fresh ideas to grow, we will not close the door and remain within a stagnant world, but will weather the period in faith and hope.

Intelligenece does not necessarily bring us to truth about ourselves. Honesty, prayerfulness, consistency, faithfulness, humor, and perseverance do.

If laughter is generally good medicine, then warmly laughing at ourselves and those instances when we start to venerate our own way of dealing with life must be especially good medicine.

If we fail to work on a philosophy of life, then our thoughts and actions will lead us into unnecessary extra mazes rather than down life's paths with their own natural curves and turns. Life is tough enough without making further trouble for ourselves by not living with a growing sense of purpose and recognition of the personal implications of Christ's death, resurrection, and life of ministry.

Boredom comes from failing to see the community of life within ourselves, and ourselves as part of God's community.

When our personality style and defenses become exaggerated our uniqueness becomes deformity.

Politeness with others does not mean acceptance of others.

When things seem to be going well, change and honest reflection are often neglected.

Is my sensitivity to others fired by true concern, or fear of rejection?

Am I embracing challenges that are character-building or ones that are personally destructive?

When we seek to become better Christians, we can do it either by focusing on our sinful illness or the positive grace we have received from God.

The heat of the fire of Christian hope doesn't totally remove the cold disappointment of its present incomplete fulfillment.

Spirituality is the essence of the Gestalt of life.

In Chinese, two characters are used to write the word for "crisis"; one symbol represents "danger," the other stands for "opportunity."

Worrying about our lack of impact on the problems of others can just as easily lead to burnout as it can to personal salvation; the difference lies in whether the expectations we have of ourselves are realistic or not.

Enlightenment doesn't always initially lead to peace, but it always leads to truth, which is the cornerstone of real satisfaction.

Where does responsibility to act end and leaving things in God's hands begin?

How are the things that annoy me in life linked to something basic in my personality?

Do I meet people interpersonally where they are, or where *I* feel they *should* be?

What are my key defensive and avoidance strategies? In what types of situations do they often come into play?

What subjects do I feel uncomfortable speaking about with others.

Which of my expectations are fired by *my* needs, and which are fired by the need to follow Christ?

What are the barriers to loving myself?

Is my mind a masochistic problem-seeking one or a courageous challenge-seeking one?

Am I as open to others as I expect them to be open to me?

Why is it that we sometimes let the praise we receive slip through our fingers, but hold on to criticism until our knuckles turn white?

Have I recently challenged my basic assumptions about life, or are they entrenched forever?

When does my uniqueness worry me and make me feel alone, and when does it give me a sense of being a special creation of God?